Seasonal Storytime Crafts

Kathryn Totten

UpstartBooks

Fort Atkinson, Wisconsin

Published by **UpstartBooks**
W5527 Highway 106
P.O. Box 800
Fort Atkinson, Wisconsin 53538-0800
1-800-448-4887

The paper used in this publication meets the minimum requirements of American National Standard for Information Science — Permanence of Paper for Printed Library Material. ANSI/NISO Z39.48-1992.

Library of Congress Cataloging-in-Publication Data
Totten, Kathryn, 1955-
  Seasonal storytime crafts / Kathryn Totten.
     p. cm.
Includes bibliographical references and index.
  ISBN 1-57950-075-7 (alk. paper)
  1. Storytelling. 2. Nature craft. 3. Creative activities and seat
work. 4. Children–Books and reading. I. Title.
  LB1042 .T65 2002
  372.67'7–dc21
                        2002008247

Acknowledgments

Thank you to my associates who suggested books and gave me advice about the Rest Activities: Virginia Brace, Lisa Cole, Carolyn Pickett, Dee Requa and Sabrina Speight.

Contents

Introduction

The purpose of this book is to make it easier to plan creative storytimes based on the seasonal themes. Each theme consists of a suggested list of picture books, rest activities that are traditional or original, songs and rhymes, and simple craft activities. These storytime plans are most suitable for children ages two to six. However, children over age six may enjoy many of the longer stories.

How to Use This Book

This book is divided into themed programs. Each theme begins with an introductory activity intended to interest and focus the attention of the children. Personalizing this introduction will help form a bond between you and your regular storytime attendees. Each theme also contains an annotated book list and several rest activities. From these you may select those that appeal to you most, keeping in mind the audience for whom you are preparing. For children ages two and three, it is usually best to select books with only one or two sentences on a page, with large and colorful illustrations, and a very familiar subject. For children ages four to six, you may select a book with a more complex story and more text. The rest activities will be essential in a storytime for children two years old. They will be welcome additions to a storytime for children ages four to six. Personalize your storytime by adding rhymes, games and fingerplays that are your favorites and by including new picture books or old favorites that come to mind as you plan. For variety, you may try telling a story as part of your presentation. The next section, Storytelling to Young Children, provides suggestions on how to select and prepare a story to tell. It includes the text of a few stories that will fit into these seasonal themes.

Storytime Strategies

Experienced storytellers who work with young children use a number of simple strategies to improve the effectiveness of their programs. After introducing the theme, it is good practice to begin by reading the longest book on the program. Doing this while the children are fresh ensures that they will remain attentive for the entire book. Some storytellers invite the children to make comments after each book is read. This allows children to practice verbal skills and can help to build their vocabulary. It also helps to foster a feeling of unity in the audience. A rest activity helps to involve and refocus the children. Allowing the children to move their bodies in an organized way will reduce their tendency to move in a disorganized way. If the rest activities start with loud noises and large motions, then become quiet and still, this prepares the children for the next book. In a 30-minute storytime you may read up to three stories, depending upon their length and the general mood of the children on that particular day. It is always acceptable to delete something that was planned if necessary. The children may want a particular book repeated, and often they want to repeat the rest activities several times. The goals are to provide an exposure to literature, a warm social experience, and a positive association with the storyteller and the library.

Crafts

The last activity of a storytime should be the craft. The crafts that are included in this book require a minimum of preparation time, and they are easy for the children to complete. There are many good reasons for including crafts with story programs. Taking a craft home after storytime gives children an opportunity to discuss with their families the books that were read that day. The craft may be made as a gift for someone else, or it may hang in the child's room or on the refrigerator as a reminder of the pleasant library experience. Many children find a 30-minute storytime to be very long. A craft activity is a welcome diversion. Crafts strengthen motor skills and help prepare children for writing and other school activities.

Storytelling to Young Children

Oral storytelling provides enrichment and entertainment for children of all ages, even the two year olds. It provides them with a good oral communication model and exposes them to a variety of inflections in human speech. It increases their ability to listen, follow and imagine as they hear a story being told. It shows them that stories are not confined to books, locked away until the children acquire the ability to read. Stories are something that can be remembered and shared even by very young children.

Creating a Story

Some storytellers are comfortable telling a spontaneous story. A character is selected, named and placed in a setting. The character is given a problem to solve. The character draws on his strengths and sometimes overcomes his fears or weaknesses in solving the problem. This can all be done in a very few sentences and can be very enjoyable for the storyteller and the children.

Original stories may be created from traditional nursery rhymes. In the rhyme, the character is given and he performs an action. The storyteller may explore what happened before, what happens next, or who else is present. This kind of story can help the children memorize the nursery rhyme, especially if it is repeated several times in the story.

Telling a Folktale

Cultural values have been preserved in stories that have been handed down orally for generations. Written versions of these folktales are excellent sources for storytellers. Folktales have been well-shaped by years of telling. This structure makes them easy to learn. A suitable story for a young audience will fit many of the following criteria:

- It can be told in five minutes or less,
- It has a repetitive phrase,
- It is cumulative,
- It appeals to the storyteller.

The stories in the next section are short folktales that are suitable for two or more of the seasonal storytime themes. Spending some time browsing in the 398.2 section of the library should provide many more. I have re-told these stories here in my own words. You may want to compare this version to other versions in print and create your own story to tell.

Using Visual Aids

When telling stories to young children, many storytellers find it helpful to use something visual to illustrate the story. Flannel board figures, simple costumes, toys or puppets are excellent visual aids. The use of a visual aid helps to stimulate the imagination of young children. A seasonal decoration may be the right place to start when selecting visual aids for the themes in this book. These may include toys, wall hangings, ceramic figures, centerpieces and candles. They are easily obtained, are colorful, and may have a lot of character.

Practice

Unless creating a spontaneous story, storytellers rely on planning and practice for a successful storytelling experience. There is something about hearing one's own voice telling the story that elicits creative ideas for gestures, postures, inflections and expressions. All of these elements can be rehearsed, which makes them come easily during the telling of the story. Working with the visual aids before using them in storytime is reassuring, also. With this preparation in place, storytellers often find themselves improvising gestures and finding delightful new phrases during their performance. These gifts only come when the storyteller is ready for them.

The Little White House

A Cumulative Tale

This is the little white house at the end of the road.

This is the porch on the little white house at the end of the road.

This is the clay pot on the porch on the little white house at the end of the road.

This is the bird that built a nest in the clay pot on the porch on the little white house at the end of the road.

This is the rabbit, which stopped to rest with his friend, the bird, who built a nest, in the clay pot on the porch on the little white house at the end of the road.

This is the butterfly that sat on the nose, of a fluffy rabbit in repose. The rabbit, which stopped to rest with his friend, the bird, who built a nest, in the clay pot on the porch of the little white house at the end of the road.

This is the gardener, gentle and kind, who asked the bird, "Do you mind if I plant this flower in the clay pot on the porch on the little white house at the end of the road?"

Then butterfly, rabbit and bird, all three, moved the nest to the willow tree, the tree near the porch on the little white house at the end of the road.

Read More About It!

Here are two more examples of cumulative stories. You may find these stories good for telling or for reading aloud.

Van Laan, Nancy. *This Is the Hat: A Story In Rhyme.* Joy Street Books, 1992. Cumulative verses follow an old man's hat as it becomes a home for a spider, mouse, and other creatures before returning to its rightful owner.

Harley, Bill. *Sitting Down To Eat.* August House Little Folk, 1996. In this cumulative story, a young boy agrees to share his snack with an ever-growing menagerie of animals; each insisting that there is room for one more.

Related Story Themes

You can use this story for the following themes in this book: Birds, Flowers and Trees, Bunnies and Bugs and Insects.

Two Goats On the Bridge

Russian Folktale

Once, long ago, two goats lived high in the mountains. One goat lived on the Blue Mountain Peak. The other goat lived on the Gray Mountain Peak. Between the two peaks was a narrow bridge.

The goats visited back and forth, as neighbors do. Some days the goat on the Blue Mountain Peak crossed over the bridge to graze on the Gray Mountain Peak. While he was there he told stories of high adventure and danger bravely met at home on his Blue Mountain Peak.

Other days the goat on the Gray Mountain Peak crossed over the bridge to graze on the Blue Mountain Peak. This goat also had many stories to tell about the storms that fell suddenly on Gray Mountain, and of possible treasures hidden in a cave there.

After some time, the goats were more than neighbors. They were friends. But one day, the two goats began to cross the bridge at the same time. They met in the middle of the bridge.

"My friend," said one, "we are at an impasse."

"That is true," said the other. "I do not want to back up."

"I will not back up, either. What shall we do?"

Head to head, horns to horns and beard to beard, the goats stared at each other for over an hour. Neither of them had an idea how to solve their problem. The longer they stared at each other, the more stubborn each became. Neither goat would back up. It appeared they would be on that bridge all day and all night.

"Have I ever told you about the time..." began the goat from Gray Mountain Peak, when he grew tired of staring silently at his friend. When his story was finished, the goat from Blue Mountain Peak told one. They traded stories until the sky turned pink and gold in the setting sun.

"I have an idea," said one. "If we are both very careful..."

"Yes, yes," said the other. "The bridge is very narrow, but..."

"We could pass without falling if we try."

"We can try."

So the goats cautiously squeezed past, each careful not to push the other off the bridge. Just as the sun set, they each crossed the bridge to land.

"Friend," called the goat from Blue Mountain Peak. "You are welcome to stay in my home tonight."

"Thank you. I will. Please make yourself at home at my place. See you in the morning?"

So each goat had a little vacation in the home of the other that night, and each goat went to sleep thinking, "He is the most agreeable goat I know."

Read More About It!

Another version of this story can be found in: *Peace Tales: World Folktales to Talk About* by Margaret Read MacDonald. Linnet Books, 1992.

Related Story Themes

You can use this story for the following themes in this book: I Love My Friends and Vacation.

Why Dogs Hate Cats

African-American Folktale

A long time ago, all the animals of the earth were friends. Dog and Cat were the best friends of all. They spent their days roaming through the grassy meadows, napping in the warm sun, or gazing up at the stars in the evening sky. Every bit of food they had, they shared. Their favorite food of all was ham.

One day Dog and Cat were chasing mice out of a man's barn. They were doing it just for fun, but the man was so happy to have his barn cleared of mice that he gave them a ham. It was a big ham, and it was so heavy that Dog and Cat had to take turns carrying it home.

The Dog carried it first. As he walked down the lane, he began to sing a song. "Our ham! Our ham! Our ham! Our ham!" It sounded almost like howling at the moon.

When it was Cat's turn to carry the ham, he made up a song to sing as well. Cat's song sounded like meowing. "My ham. My ham. My ham. My ham."

When it was Dog's turn to carry it again, he sang, "Our ham. Our ham. Our ham. Our ham."

Cat took his turn next, singing, "My ham. My ham. My ham. My ham."

Finally Dog asked, "Cat, why is it that you sing 'My ham'? It is our ham, isn't it?"

Cat pretended not to hear. Cat continued to sing, "My ham. My ham. My ham. My ham," until he came to a bend in the road, where it went around a big tree. Quick as lightning, Cat ran up the tree, sat down on a limb, and ate the whole ham. Dog could not believe it! His best friend ate their ham. Dog could not climb up the tree, but he stood below snarling and barking at Cat.

"I cannot get you now, Cat, but you will have to come down from that tree sometime, and when you do, I will be waiting. I'll chase you until your whiskers turn gray!"

That is the reason why every time a dog sees a cat, he chases it. He is still mad about the ham.

Read More About It!

Another version of this story can be found in: *The Knee-High Man and Other Tales* by Julius Lester. Dial Books for Young Readers, 1972.

Related Story Themes

You can use this story for the following themes in this book: Thanksgiving Feast and Delicious Treats.

The Big, Fat, Hairy Toe

Traditional American Folktale

Once upon a time, a woman lived in a little house in the country with her little boy. The woman was poor, but she managed to feed her little boy by growing potatoes in a little garden behind the house.

When it was time to cook dinner she went out to the little garden with her cooking pot and a shovel.

She dug in the dirt, and she pulled potatoes up. She dug in the dirt, and she pulled potatoes up. She dug in the dirt, and she pulled potatoes up until her pot was full.

One day she dug up a very unusual potato. "Why, it looks just like a BIG, FAT, HAIRY TOE!" she said.

It was so big, she didn't dig up any more potatoes that day. The woman took it home and made potato soup for supper. Her little boy ate a big bowl of potato soup with a slurp, slurp, slurp. Then he had a bath and she tucked him in bed.

The woman was sitting by the fire, knitting a sweater, when she heard a strange sound. It was a voice, but is sounded very faint, very far away. The voice said,

"I want my BIG, FAT, HAIRY TOE!"

The woman was scared, so she went to the door and fastened the latch. She went to the windows and pulled the shutters closed. She went to the fireplace and put on another log, and then she went to bed.

She pulled the covers up to her chin, and little by little she got sleepy. She was almost asleep when she heard the strange sound again. It was the voice, a little louder, and a little closer. The voice said,

"I want my BIG, FAT, HAIRY TOE!"

The woman was really scared now. She got up from bed and checked the door latch. She went to the windows and checked the shutters. She went to the fireplace and put on two more logs, and then she went to bed.

She pulled the covers up to her chin, and trembled. She didn't know who or what it was that kept saying,

"I want my BIG, FAT, HAIRY TOE!"

She was beginning to feel sleepy when once again, she heard the voice. This time it was very loud, and sounded like it was right outside her house! The voice said,

"I want my BIG, FAT, HAIRY TOE!"

The woman jumped out of bed, she ran to the kitchen, she grabbed the pot of potato soup. Then she ran to the door, opened the latch and threw the pot out into the yard.

"Take it!" she yelled, then she ran back to bed. She never, ever made potato soup again.

Notes on Telling the Story

Several actions that can be pantomimed in this story such as digging in the garden, knitting, fastening doors and windows, and pulling up the covers. Each time the words "I want my BIG, FAT, HAIRY TOE!" are said, a gesture should be performed in a manner that comes easily to you. Here is one suggestion. For the word "big," the arms reach up and down. For the word "fat," the arms are extended out to the sides. For the word "hairy," the fingers wiggle. For the word "toe," point to the toe.

Read More About It!

Another version of this story can be found in: Diane Goode's **Book of Scary Stories and Songs.** Dutton, 1994. It is similar to "Teeny Tiny" in: **English Fairy Tales** by Joseph Jacobs. Alfred Knopf, 1993. Also read "Tailypo" in: **Short and Shivery: Thirty Chilling Tales** by Robert D. San Souci. Doubleday, 1987.

Related Story Themes

You can use this story for the following themes in this book: St. Patrick's Day and Spooky Stories.

Why Spider Has a Little Head and a Big Bottom

Ashanti (West Africa) Folktale

One day Ananzi the Spider went out to find food for his family. He came to the river, and there he saw Elephant, Crocodile, and Turtle splashing and singing. Elephant splashed with his huge trunk. Crocodile splashed with his strong tail. Turtle climbed high up on a rock, tucked in his head, and laughed as he jumped into the river, making a huge splash with his shell. While they splashed in the water, they were singing this song:

We are splashing the river, and soon it will be dry-o.
We will have many a fish to eat before the end of day-o!

Ananzi watched them splash until a little pool in the river was dry. He saw them scoop up baskets of fish from the bottom of this dry pool. Then they went to another pool and began to splash again. Ananzi wanted some fish, too.

"I like your song. May I join you?" he asked.

"Sing," said Elephant, spraying himself with water from his trunk.

Ananzi sang along, but with his tiny feet he could not splash much. "I have nothing to splash with," he lamented.

Crocodile gave a huge smile and said, "Ananzi, I will pull off your head. You can splash with that!"

Ananzi really wanted some fish, so he allowed crocodile to pull off his head. He held it with his arms and splashed and sang with the others.

We are splashing the river, and soon it will be dry-o.
We will have many a fish to eat before the end of day-o!

Soon they had splashed all the water out of that pool in the river, and they collected many fish. Elephant gave Ananzi his share.

"Put your head back on, and go home and eat," he said. "But you must never sing that song again, or your head will fall off."

Ananzi took his basket of fish and started on the road home. He was happy. First, he bounced. Then he hummed. Then he started to sing.

We are splashing…

Ananzi cupped his hands over his mouth. "No, no, you cannot sing that song," he told himself. Once more he started down the road and that happy feeling came back. First, he bounced. Then he hummed. Then he started to sing. Before he could stop himself, he sang the whole song!

We are splashing the river, and soon it will be dry-o.
We will have many a fish to eat before the end of day-o!

Sure enough, his head fell off and rolled in the dust. Ananzi picked up his head with two of his arms, and his basket of fish with two of his arms, and went running back to the river.

"Please help me," he said.

Turtle laughed. "You sang the song, didn't you?"

Crocodile smiled. "We told you not to sing that song."

Elephant was getting a drink from the river. When he saw Ananzi he laughed so hard he sprayed water all over spider with his trunk. "I will help you," he said.

Elephant held Ananzi's head in his trunk, raised it high over his head, and brought it down with a smack against Ananzi. Unfortunately, Elephant's aim was not very good. Instead of sticking Ananzi's head back on top, he stuck it on his bottom. It was stuck for good!

"Oh well," said Ananzi. "At least I won't lose it again." Ananzi picked up his basket of fish and went home. To this very day, he has a very tiny

Notes on Telling the Story

When you sing the song in this story, create your own melody. It's fun to make your voice go high on the last "O." Sing it several times, then invite the audience to sing with you.

Read More About It!

Another version of this story can be found in: *How the People Sang the Mountains Up: How and Why Stories* by Maria Leach. Viking, 1967.

Related Story Themes

You can use this story for the following themes in this book: Picnics, Water Play and Bugs and Insects.

Storytime Themes

Starting School

Before Sharing Books

Talk about a memory from your school days, such as a game you enjoyed, a favorite teacher or learning to count. Tell the children it is almost time for stories. Ask the children to count with you to 10, then get in a comfortable position so they can listen to the stories.

Rest Activities

Songs

We Are Learning

(Sung to the tune: "Mary Had a Little Lamb")

We are learning how to count,
How to count, how to count.
We are learning how to count,
Every day at school.
Substitute: How to read, how to write, how to play, how to dance, how to draw....

The More We Get Together *(Traditional)*

The more we get together, together, together,
The more we get together the happier we'll be.
For your friends are my friends,
And my friends are your friends.
The more we get together the happier we'll be.

Action Rhyme

School Time, Bob

Bob gets up and washes his face.
(Hands on face.)
He puts on a clean shirt and tucks it in his waist.
(Tuck in shirt.)
He runs to the table and eats his toast.
(Pretend to take a bite.)
He bumps his juice and spills it, almost.
(Hands near face, look scared.)
He picks up his backpack and puts it on.
(Pretend to put on backpack.)
Kisses his Mom, and whoosh! He's gone.
(Blow a kiss.)

Books to Share

Bloom, Suzanne. *The Bus for Us.* Boyds Mills Press, 2001. On her first day of school, Tess wonders what the school bus will look like.

Bruss, Deborah. *Book! Book! Book!* Arthur A. Levine Books, 2001. When the children go back to school, the animals on the farm are bored, so they go into the library in town trying to find something to do.

Charlton, Nancy Lee. *Derek's Dog Days.* Harcourt Brace, 1996. Derek thinks he'd prefer to be a dog until he starts school and finds out it's even more fun being a boy.

Haffner, Margaret. *Fearless Jake.* Firefly Books, 1996. Armed only with his quick reflexes, courage and a powerful imagination, Jake must battle the elements, escape from dangerous creatures and get to school on time.

Wells, Rosemary. Edward *Unready for School.* Dial Books for Young Readers, 1995. Edward, a shy, young bear unready for play school, feels out of place surrounded by students who are ready, busy and happy.

Pom-pom Pencil Friend

Talk about how the start of the school year is a time for renewing old friendships and starting new ones. Then, make this simple craft.

Directions

Hot glue a 1" pom-pom to the top of a pencil. Hot glue wiggle eyes on the pom-pom. Cut a 6" piece of pipe cleaner. At storytime, the child can wrap the pipe cleaner around the pencil and twist it, making arms.

 This craft takes 5 minutes to complete.

Soon it Will Turn Cold

Before Sharing Books

Bring in a few chilly weather items of clothing, such as jackets, sweaters, scarves, hats and gloves. Try some of them on yourself, or a puppet, and explain why it is a good idea to take along something warm in the morning, even if it seems like the weather will be nice. Tell the children about a time when you forgot your jacket and were caught in the rain or a similar experience. Now have them all put on their pretend sweaters, bundle up and settle down for stories.

Rest Activities

Songs

Did You Ever See a Squirrel
(Sung to the tune: "Did You Ever See a Lassie")

Did you ever see a squirrel,
(Put hands up by face like paws.)
A squirrel, a squirrel.
Did you ever see a squirrel,
Go this way and that?
(Pretend to put nuts in mouth.)
Go this way and that way,
Go this way and that way,
Did you ever see a squirrel,
(Put hands up by face like paws.)
Go this way and that?
(Pretend to put nuts in mouth.)

I'm Going to Take a Jacket
(Sung to the tune: "For He's a Jolly Good Fellow")

I'm going to take a jacket,
I'm going to take a jacket,
I'm going to take a jacket,
When I go out today.

When I go out today,
When I go out today,

I'm going to take a jacket.
I'm going to take a jacket,
I'm going to take a jacket,
When I go out today.

Substitute sweater, hat, umbrella…

Action Rhyme

Bake a Treat

When the wind is blowing,
(Wave arms overhead.)
And the skies are getting gray,
We have to stay indoors,
It's too cold to go out to play.
(Wrap arms around body.)
We gather in the kitchen,
And let the oven heat,
(Pretend to turn on oven.)
We stir and mix, stir and mix,
(Pretend to stir cake or cookies.)
It's time to bake a treat.
(Rub tummy.)

Books to Share

Birchall, Mark. *Rabbit's Wooly Sweater.* Carolrhoda Books, 2001. Because she and her toy rabbit Mr. Cuddles always do everything together, Rabbit does not want to wear her new sweater unless he has one as well.

Saunders-Smith, Gail. *Warm Clothes.* Pebble Books, 1998. Simple text and photographs present the clothing worn to keep warm as fall changes to winter.

Sloat, Teri. *Sody Sallyratus.* Dutton Children's Books, 1997. When one after another family member goes

the store for baking soda and never returns, the pet squirrel decides to investigate in this retelling of a traditional Appalachian tale.

Stoeke, Janet Morgan. *A Hat for Minerva Louise.* Dutton Children's Books, 1994. Minerva Louise, a snow-loving chicken, mistakes a pair of mittens for two hats to keep both ends warm.

Squirrel

Tell the children that animals prepare for cold weather by growing thicker fur and storing food. Then, help them make this squirrel craft.

Directions

Copy the pattern and cut out. At storytime let the children color the squirrel and the tree. Then let them paste the squirrel in his tree home using a glue stick.

 This craft takes 10 minutes to complete.

Colorful Leaves

Before Sharing Books

Bring in some dried leaves in a variety of colors. Talk to the children about what they have seen near their homes. Discuss and compare the sizes and colors of the leaves.

Rest Activities

Song

This Is the Way We Rake the Leaves

(Sung to the tune: "Here We Go 'Round the Mulberry Bush")

This is the way we rake the leaves,
Rake the leaves, rake the leaves.
This is the way we rake the leaves,
On a chilly morning.

Poem

Favorite Fall Colors

We went for a walk,
On a crisp autumn day.
"Look! The leaves are changing,"
I heard my friend say.
I asked, "What color is your favorite?"
My friend said,
"I really like the yellow leaves."
"I like red."

Fingerplay

Five Little Leaves

Five little leaves up in a tree.
One little leaf said, "Look at me!"
The leaf let go and down he fell.
Ouch! He didn't feel so well.
(Repeat with four, three, two, one.)

Books to Share

Baxter, Nicola. *Autumn.* Children's Press, 1996. A simple discussion of various facets of autumn, including animal hibernation and migration, leaves changing colors and falling, and the Halloween holiday.

Hall, Zoe. *Fall Leaves Fall!* Scholastic, 2000. When fall comes, two brothers enjoy catching the falling leaves, stomping on them, kicking them, jumping in piles of them and using them to make pictures.

Knutson, Kimberley. *Ska-tat!* Macmillan Pub., 1993. Children describe playing in the colorful, scratchy leaves as they fall down from the trees.

Merriam, Eve. *Low Song.* Margaret K. McElderry Books, 2001. Rhyming text celebrates various aspects of the world, from falling leaves and falling snow to hushaby tunes and little new moons.

Saunders-Smith, Gail. *Autumn Leaves.* Pebble Books, 1998. Simple text and photographs present the different types and colors of leaves found in the Northern Hemisphere in autumn.

Leaf Bag

Talk about the fun of walking through crisp leaves and collecting favorites along the way. Then, make this collection bag.

Directions
Copy leaf pattern and cut out several, in different colors, for each child. At storytime let the children glue three or four leaves on a paper lunch bag, using a glue stick. They may use the bag to hold the leaves they collect on an afternoon walk.

 This craft takes 5 minutes to complete.

An Autumn Walk

Before Sharing Books

Take the children on an imaginary walk. Talk about what you see. You may mention birds that live in your area, squirrels, cats and dogs, fall decorations on houses, corn stalks, pumpkins, apples, etc. After a long walk, it is nice to sit quietly and listen to stories. When they are settled down, begin.

Rest Activities

Song

We Are Walking

(Sung to the tune: "Are You Sleeping")

We are walking. We are walking.
Far and near. Far and near.
Better take a sweater. Better take a sweater.
Fall is here. Fall is here.

Action Rhymes

Looking for Colors

(Pretend to go walking outdoors, looking at the changing colors. People are wearing warmer clothes. Homes are decorated for fall. Gardens are full of pumpkins, birds and animals. Say the rhyme that follows, then lead the children in naming a few things of that color that could be seen where you are walking. Then pretend to walk again, and say the rhyme again using another color.)

Red, yellow, brown and green.
Many colors can be seen.
What do you see that's red?
(Apples, sweater, bird, oak leaves…)

The Little Squirrel

I saw a little squirrel run up a tree.
(Arms overhead.)
He shook his little tail like that.
(Shake your tail.)
He jumped on a branch, shook the leaves.
(Jump and shake body.)
And the leaves fell down on my hat.
(Touch head.)

Books to Share

Duncan, Lois. *I Walk at Night.* Viking, 2000. A cat describes the ways in which it enjoys spending the day and night.

Laser, Michael. *The Rain.* Simon & Schuster, 1997. In the city, the town, and the forest, people enjoy the beauty of a gentle autumn rainfall.

Hazelaar, Cor. *Dogs Everywhere. Knopf, 1995.* Describes dogs being walked in the park.

Lyon, George Ella. *Counting on the Woods: A Poem.* DK Pub., 1998. Uses rhyme to enumerate and describe natural objects seen while walking through the woods.

Autumn Walk Book

After storytime, encourage children to go for a walk, looking for the items in their book.

My Autumn Walk Book

Directions
Copy the pattern and cut out. Staple the pages together to make a booklet. Let the children color the pictures.

 This craft takes 5 minutes to complete.

Owls

Before Sharing Books

Have the children close their eyes and cover them with their hands. Keeping their eyes covered, have them open their eyes, and notice how dark it seems. Tell them some animals can see well in the dark. Ask them to name some animals that like to come out after dark. When they name owls, ask them to pretend they are baby owls sitting in their nests, ready for stories.

Rest Activities

Song

Wise Old Owl

(Sung to the tune: "Twinkle, Twinkle Little Star")

Wise old owl wakes up at night.
Fluffs his feathers out just right.
Moonlight shines and makes him blink.
Breezes blow and make him think.
"What a lucky owl am I.
I can spread my wings and fly!"

Fingerplays

Run Away Mice

Two little mice went out to play.
(Hold up two fingers.)
One saw an owl. It gave him a fright.
(Look scared.)
He said, "It's not safe to play at night.
(Shake head.)
Run away! Run away! Run away!"
(Hands behind back.)

Four Gray Owls

Four gray owls sat in a tree.
(Hold up four fingers.)
One flew away and then there were three.
(Flap arms.)
Three gray owls called, "Who, who, who."
(Hold up three fingers, place hands by mouth.)
One flew away and then there were two.
(Flap arms.)
Two gray owls saw a mouse on the run.
(Hold up two fingers, make fingers run up arm.)
One flew away, and then there was one.
(Flap arms.)
One gray owl gave a yawn.
(Hold up one finger, yawn.)
Closed his eyes and napped until dawn.
(Rest face on hands as if sleeping.)

Books to Share

Crebbin, June. *Fly by Night.* Candlewick Press, 1993. A young owl eagerly awaits the nighttime to make his first flight with his mother.

Ezra, Mark. *The Frightened Little Owl.* Crocodile Books, 1997. Although afraid to fly, Little Owl leaves the safety of her nest and goes to look for her missing mother, who has been watching over her all the time.

Hayes, Sarah. *This is the Bear and the Scary Night.* Candlewick Press, 1998. After a boy leaves his teddy bear in a park, it grows dark; then the bear suffers a terrible fright when an owl swoops him up into the night.

Johnston, Tony. *The Barn Owls.* Charlesbridge, 2000. For at least 100 years, generations of barn owls have slept, hunted, called, raised their young and glided silently above the wheat fields around an old barn.

Owl In a Nest

Talk about how owls nest in large holes in old trees. Then, have children each make their own owl and nest.

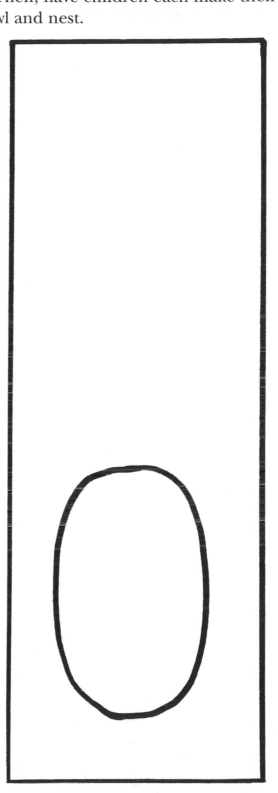

Directions

Copy the pattern and cut out. Fold the tree pattern in half. At storytime the children may color the owl, then open the tree and paste the owl on it, so that he shows through when the tree is closed again. This puts the owl in his nest.

 This craft takes 10 minutes to complete.

Pumpkins

Before Sharing Books

Set out an assortment of pumpkins. Ask the children to count them. Ask them to point to the biggest one, the smallest one, the darkest one, the tallest one, etc.

Rest Activities

Song

Pumpkin Time

(Sung to the tune: "Row, Row, Row Your Boat")

Pum, pum, pumpkin time,
Pumpkin pumpkin time,
Pumpkin pumpkin pumpkin pumpkin,
Pumpkin pumpkin time.

(Sing it slowly, then faster and faster until everyone is giggling.)

Action Story

Scared Pumpkins

This little pumpkin says, "I heard a noise."
(Wiggle thumb.)
This little pumpkin says, "I'm afraid."
(Wiggle index finger.)
This little pumpkin says, "Let's run away."
(Wiggle middle finger.)
This little pumpkin says, "I don't have any feet."
(Wiggle ring finger.)
This little pumpkin says, "Roll!"
(Wiggle little finger, roll hands very fast.)

Fingerplay

The Little Pumpkin's Wish

I'm a little pumpkin big and round.
(Hold arms out in a circle.)
Here is my wiggly vine.
(Wiggle hand on top of head.)
I hope the children will pick me.
(Point to self.)
When it's jack-o'-lantern time.
(Big smile.)

Books to Share

Bunting, Eve. *The Pumpkin Fair.* Clarion Books, 1997. A rather ordinary pumpkin wins a prize for "the best-loved pumpkin at the fair, the best-loved pumpkin anywhere."

Cooper, Helen. *Pumpkin Soup.* Farrar Straus Giroux, 1999. The Cat and the Squirrel come to blows with the Duck in arguing about who will perform what duty in preparing their pumpkin soup, and they almost lose the Duck's friendship when he decides to leave them.

Moore, Elaine. *Grandma's Smile.* Lothrop, Lee & Shepard Books, 1995. Kim's grandmother's smile is the inspiration for the jack-o'-lantern face she draws on her pumpkin at a fall festival.

Scott, C. Anne. *Old Jake's Skirts.* Northland Pub., 1998. A reclusive pumpkin farmer finds an abandoned steamer trunk filled with cotton calico skirts, which he eventually uses around the house in ways which seem to bring him luck.

Zagwyn, Deborah Turney. *The Pumpkin Blanket.* Tricycle Press, 1997. A little girl sacrifices her beloved blanket to save the pumpkins in the garden from frost.

Dog in a Pumpkin

Make this peek-a-boo craft for a unique Halloween activity.

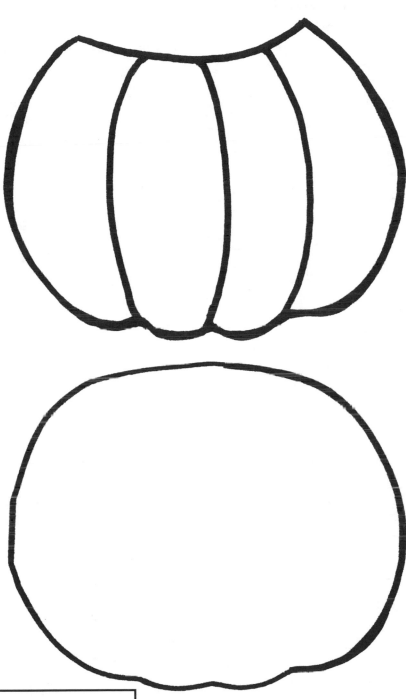

Directions

Copy the pattern and cut out. Paste the pumpkin pieces together along the edges, leaving the top open. At story-time the children may color the pumpkin and the dog. They may then slide the dog inside the pumpkin so that the pumpkin lid closes. By pulling up the lid they may show the dog who is hiding in the pumpkin.

 This craft takes 10 minutes to complete.

Dressing Up

Before Sharing Books

Bring a variety of odd hats, capes, and other costume accessories to storytime. Try them on one by one, asking for the children to help you decide what to wear for Halloween. Try them on in funny ways—the more unusual, the better. For example, put a skirt on your head for a wig.

Rest Activities

Action Rhyme

What Will You Be?

Oh, what will you be for Halloween,
When everyone dresses up?
Will you be something scary,
(Make a scary face.)
Or a beautiful fairy?
(Dance.)
Will you wear a tall hat,
(Hands on head.)
Will you make yourself fat,
(Arms out in a circle.)
Tell me, what will you be?
(Point to a person near you.)

Rhyme

Create a Costume

Make-up, mask, wig, cape,
Sheet, shoes, hat, drape,
Pin it. Tie it. Think. Create.
To make your costume really great.

Fingerplay

Halloween Parade

(As you put up one finger at a time from one to ten, name the following, and make the appropriate noise.)

One Black Cat *(Meow.)*
Two Scary Ghosts *(Boo.)*
Three Beauty Queens *(Giggle.)*
Four Dinosaurs *(Roar.)*
Five Skeletons *(Rattle.)*
Six Hairy Monsters *(Grrr.)*
Seven Silly Clowns *(Beep nose.)*
Eight Black Spiders *(EEK!)*
Nine Green Dragons *(Fire!)*
Ten Aliens *(Oooo!)*

Books to Share

Greene, Carol. *The 13 Days of Halloween.* Troll/Bridgewater Books, 2000. A Halloween version of "The Twelve Days of Christmas," featuring such seasonal gifts as bats, goblins, spiders, worms and ghosts.

Rockwell, Anne F. *Halloween Day.* HarperCollins, 1997. The ten preschoolers in Mrs. Madoff's class wear their Halloween costumes to school, filling the room with a cat, a pirate, a witch and other characters.

Shaw, Nancy. *Sheep Trick or Treat.* Houghton Mifflin, 1997. When sheep dress up to go trick-or-treating at a nearby farm, their costumes scare away some wolves lurking in the woods.

Sweeney, Jacqueline. *Who Said Boo?* Benchmark Books/Marshall Cavendish, 2000. Animal friends enjoy dressing up in scary Halloween costumes and going out into the dark night for a party given in Owl Woods.

Dress the Ghost

Everyone knows that dressing up as a ghost is a common Halloween costume. But, what do ghosts wear for trick-or-treating?

Directions
Copy the pattern and cut out. At storytime, let the children color the ghost face, boots, mittens, tie and bat, then paste them on the ghost.

 This craft takes 10 minutes to complete.

Spooky Stories

Before Sharing Books

Tell the children about something that frightened you, such as a noise in your garage or a spider in a corner of your house. Tell the children you want to learn how to be brave. Tell them you believe it will help if you read spooky stories.

Rest Activities

Song

Tell Me a Story

(Sung to the tune: "Go Tell Aunt Rhody")

Tell me a story, tell me a story,
Tell me a story,
The scariest one you know.

Action Story

Four Little Ghosts

Four little ghosts, on a dare,
(Hold up four fingers.)
Went out to find someone to scare.
(Make a scary face.)
They said, "Boo" and the cat said, "Hiss."
(Pretend to stroke cat whiskers.)
They said, "Boo" and the dog said, "Yowl!"
(Pant like a dog.)
They said, "Boo" and the bat flew away.
(Make hand fly like a bat.)
They said, "Boo" and the bear climbed a tree.
(Hand over hand, as if climbing.)

They said, "Boo" and I said "Hey!"
(Hands on hips.)
"Don't come back until Halloween Day."
(Shake finger and shout!)

Poem

I Can Be Brave

I can be brave,
Unless I'm in the noisy woods,
Or in a dark, damp cave.
I can be bold,
Unless I'm in a haunted house,
Where spooky stories are told.
I never cry,
Unless a spider crawls on me,
Or a bat flies by.

Books to Share

Andrews, Sylvia. *Rattlebone Rock.* HarperCollins, 1995. When skeletons, ghouls, witches and assorted other spooky creatures take up the rock beat, a town has its best-ever Halloween.

Huck, Charlotte S. *A Creepy Countdown.* Greenwillow Books, 1998. Ten scary Halloween things, such as jack-o'-lanterns, bats, and witches, count from one to ten and then back down again.

Martin, Bill. *A Beasty Story.* Silver Whistle/Harcourt Brace, 1999. A group of mice venture into a dark, dark woods where they find a dark brown house with a dark red stair leading past other dark colors to a spooky surprise.

Talbott, Hudson. *O'Sullivan Stew: A Tale Cooked Up in Ireland.* Putnam's, 1999. When the witch of Crookhaven, a village on the zigzagging coast of Ireland, has her horse stolen by the King and strikes back with famine and disaster, Kate decides to save the day by getting the horse back for her.

Washington, Donna. *A Big, Spooky House.* Hyperion Books for Children, 2000. On his way to join the army, the big strong man of the village, who is scared of nothing, spends the night in a spooky house where a series of ever-larger cats ask him the same unusual question.

Witch Silhouette

Children can take this haunting craft home with them!

Directions
Copy the witch pattern on colored paper and cut out. Suggested colors are: orange, brown, gray or black. Copy the moon on yellow paper and cut out. At storytime the children can paste the witch on the moon.

 This craft takes 5 minutes to complete.

Horses

Before Sharing Books

Invite the children to stand and join the herd of wild horses. After deciding what color and size of horse they want to be, it is time to run! Start off slowly patting your lap with your hands. Ask the children to do the same. As you run faster, the sound gets faster and louder. Slow down. Cool down. Time for a rest. Everyone can now sit down and enjoy horse stories.

Rest Activities

Song

All the Pretty Little Horses (*Traditional*)

Hush-a-bye, don't you cry.
Go to sleepy little baby.
When you wake, you shall have,
All the pretty little horses.
Dapples and grays, pintos and bays,
All the pretty little horses.

Action Rhyme

I Am a Horse

I wake up in the barn, (*Stand up.*)
I smell the hay, (*Take a deep breath.*)
I eat my oats, (*Pretend to eat.*)
I go out to play. (*Push open the gate.*)
I run like the wind, (*Run fast in place.*)
I leap and dance, (*Turn around.*)
My boy rides me, (*Point to back.*)
When he has a chance.
At the end of the day,
(*Paw the ground with your foot.*)
I'm happy of course, (*Big smile.*)
Nothing is better, (*Shake head.*)
Than being a horse. (*Whinny like a horse.*)

Rhyme

Trot, Trot to Boston (*Traditional*)

Trot, trot to Boston to buy a fat pig.
Home again, home again, jiggity jig.
Trot, trot to Boston to buy a fat hog.
Home again, home again, joggity jog.

Books to Share

Appelt, Kathi. *The Thunderherd.* Morrow Junior Books, 1996. A lone mustang joins with a wild herd as it runs down the mountainside to a grassy prairie.

Chandra, Deborah. *A Is for Amos.* Farrar Straus Giroux, 1999. A rider on Amos goes around the farm and back home to the barn finding all the letters of the alphabet.

Damrell, Liz. *With the Wind.* Orchard Books, 1991. A lyrical celebration of the power and majesty of horses and horseback riding.

Mullins, Patricia. *One Horse Waiting for Me.* Simon & Schuster Book for Young Readers, 1998. A rhymed counting book from one to twelve celebrates horses, real and imaginary.

Tiny Stick Horse

After children imagine themselves to be horses, have them create their own herd!

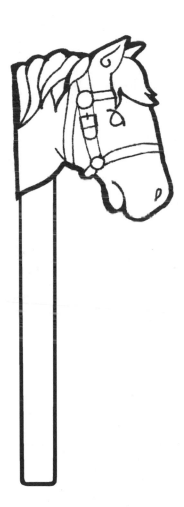

Directions

Copy the pattern and cut out. At storytime the children can color the horse head, then paste it to a craft stick using a glue stick.

 This craft takes 10 minutes to complete.

Thanksgiving Feast

Before Sharing Books

Spread a tablecloth out, and set a nice place setting. Ask the children to pretend it is time for a holiday feast. What is on the table? Take suggestions from them for a few minutes. Now that everyone is full, it is time for a story.

Rest Activities

Song

I Love Pie

(Sung to the tune: "Three Blind Mice")

I love pie. I love pie.
Eat 'til I die. Eat 'til I die.
Pumpkin, apple, cherry, peach.
Please give me a slice of each.
Pie is my favorite kind of treat.
I love pie.

Action Story

Stuff the Turkey

(This is a call and response story. You may use as many foods as you wish, and call out the "What do you do" line. The children respond with "Stuff the turkey" and they pretend to eat. When you ask "Who is the turkey?" everyone points to self and shouts "Me!")

What do you do with the rolls and butter?
Stuff the turkey!
What do you do with the green bean casserole?
Stuff the turkey!
What do you do with the mashed potatoes?
Stuff the turkey!

What do you do with the pickles and olives?
Stuff the turkey!
Who is the turkey?
Me!

Fingerplay

Turkey Runs Away

(For this fingerplay, an open hand will take the part of the turkey. The thumb is the turkey's head, the fingers are his feathers, and the palm is his body. You may want to draw a face on your thumb, or make a glove puppet that looks like a turkey.)

Turkey, Turkey, wake up and stretch.
(Open hand wide.)
Turkey, Turkey, wiggle your feathers.
(Wiggle fingers.)
Turkey, Turkey, company is coming.
(Turn hand.)
Turkey, Turkey, do you smell dinner cooking?
(Sniff.)
Turkey, Turkey, ran away.
(Hand behind back.)

Books to Share

Carlson, Nancy L. *A Visit to Grandma's.* Puffin, 1993. When Tina and her parents go to spend Thanksgiving with Grandma in her new Florida condominium, they are surprised to find that she is very different from when she lived on the farm.

Child, Lydia Maria Francis. *Over the River and Through the Wood.* Henry Holt, 1996. An illustrated version of the poem that became a well-known song about a journey through the snow to grandfather's house for Thanksgiving dinner.

Nikola-Lisa, W. *1, 2, 3 Thanksgiving!* A. Whitman, 1991. A Thanksgiving counting book depicting the numbers one through ten through scenes of the holiday.

Pomeranc, Marion Hess. *The Can-do Thanksgiving.* A. Whitman, 1998. Dee experiences excitement and satisfaction when she helps prepare and serve food for the needy at a church on Thanksgiving.

Turkey Cup-Hugger

After talking about a grand feast, children will be glad to have a treat! Serve small candies or raisins to fill their cups.

Directions
Copy the pattern and cut out. At storytime the children may color the turkey, then wrap his wings around a three-ounce paper cup and paste in place. The cup may be filled with candy corn or other treat, if desired.

 This craft takes 10 minutes to complete.

Family Togetherness

Before Sharing Books

Make several sets of paper dolls in various sizes and colors to display on your table. (To do this, fold a piece of paper accordion fold, draw a doll with hands and feet on the fold, and cut out. When it is opened the dolls are connected as if holding hands.) Discuss the differences and similarities in the doll families. They have different numbers of family members, they each have a unique look, but they each are a family

Rest Activities

Songs

Fill Me Up

(Sung to the tune: "Build Me Up Buttercup")

Why don't you fill me up,
Fill me up, Granny.
Pass the veggie plate.
The turkey tastes great.
And best of all,
Best of all, Granny,
Are the candied yams
Or maybe the ham.
I can eat more than anyone, Granny.
You know I'm a growing child.
So fill me up, Granny,
Or I'll turn wild.

Fingerplay

Family Togetherness

The family gets together at holiday time.
(Hold up both hands.)
The cousins, aunts and uncles all get in line.
(Touch each finger.)

Everybody kisses me, and that's just fine.
(Kiss palm of one hand, then the other.)
Everybody has a real good time. *(Wiggle fingers.)*

Action Rhyme

Telephone Invitations

Mommy's on the phone.
(Pretend to talk on phone.)
She's calling Uncle John.
(Hold hand up high, indicating his height.)
Come over, come over,
(Motion toward self with hand.)
And *(clap)* he comes.
(Repeat the same actions with the following verses. Or, make up additional verses on your own.)

Mommy's on the phone.
She's calling Aunt LouAnn.
Come over, come over,
And *(Clap.)* she comes.

Mommy's on the phone.
She's calling Gramps and Gran.
Come over, come over,
And *(Clap.)* they come.

Books to Share

Bullard, Lisa. *Not Enough Beds! A Christmas Alphabet Book.* Carolrhoda Books, 1999. Zachary goes through the alphabet recounting who sleeps where, from Aunt Alison in an overstuffed chair to himself under the tree, when all the relatives come to visit at Christmas.

Caseley, Judith. *Mickey's Class Play.* Greenwillow Books, 1998. With the help of his family, Mickey enjoys being a duck in his class play.

Falwell, Cathryn. *Feast for 10.* Clarion Books, 1993. Numbers from one to ten are used to tell how a family shops and works together to prepare a meal.

Joosse, Barbara M. *Snow Day!* Clarion Books, 1995. When school is cancelled because of snow, Robby and his family enjoy the day together.

Zamorano, Ana. *Let's Eat!* Scholastic, 1997. Each day Antonio's Mama tries to get everyone to sit down together to eat, but someone is always busy elsewhere, until the family celebrates a new arrival.

Gingerbread Family

Talk about the different kinds of families and what all families have in common. Then, help children make gingerbread families to take with them.

Directions
Copy the pattern and cut out several for each child. At storytime the children may color the gingerbread people, one for each member of their family. Then they may paste them on a paper plate using a glue stick.

 This craft takes 10 minutes to complete.

Grandparents

Before Sharing Books

Bring some items that remind you of older folks, such as a quilt, an old kitchen utensil or gardening tool, a pair of boots, a flower vase, a piece of jewelry. Hold up each item, tell its purpose and share a memory connected with the item. Ask the children if they are ready to hear some stories about children and their grandparents.

Rest Activities

Rhymes

Grandma and Grandpa Come to Visit
When Grandma comes to visit,
We like to play with toys.
(Pretend to stack blocks.)
We read a book, and sing some songs.
(Pretend to hold a book in hands.)
That's what she enjoys.
(Smile, point to face.)

When Grandpa comes to visit,
He likes to tickle me.
(Pretend to tickle your tummy.)
We take a walk, then I jump up,
(Walk in place.)
And grandpa carries me.
(Bend over, then jump up.)

There Was An Old Woman *(Traditional)*

There was an old woman who lived in a shoe.
She had so many children; she didn't know what
  to do.
She gave them some broth, without any bread.
She hugged them all sweetly, and sent them to
  bed.

Game

Grandma May I *(Adapted traditional game)*
Children stand up in a line against a wall. You stand at the opposite wall. Give them a suggested step, such as "Take three bunny hops." The children must ask, "Grandma May I" before they move, then they take the suggested step. Continue play until all of the children reach you.

Books to Share

Carlson, Nancy L. *Hooray for Grandparent's Day.* Viking, 2000. Arnie doesn't have grandparents to come to school on Grandparent's Day, but it turns out he has a lot of people who can substitute.

Darling, Benjamin. *Valerie and the Silver Pear.* Four Winds Press, 1992. Valerie and her grandfather preserve the memory of her grandmother by making pear pies together. Includes a recipe for pear pie.

Haas, Jessie. *Hurry!* Greenwillow Books, 2000. A young girl helps her grandparents get the hay in before a rainstorm ruins the crop.

Koralek, Jenny. *Night Ride to Nanna's.* Candlewick Press, 2000. A young girl describes the special things she sees when her family makes a nighttime trip to her grandparents' house.

Schneider, Antonie. The Birthday Bear. North-South Books, 1996. David and his sister Sally get a surprise visitor when they celebrate his birthday in the country with Grandma and Grandpa.

Grandma and Grandpa Snow People

These cute decorations make great gifts for Grandma and Grandpa.

Directions

Copy the pattern and cut out. Cut an 8" piece of yarn, tie it to form a loop, and tape or glue it to the back of each snow person. At storytime the children may color one of each. The snow people may be used as a tree ornament or window decoration.

 This craft takes 10 minutes to complete.

Delicious Treats

Before Sharing Books

Bring baking tools, such as measuring cups, wooden spoons, mixing bowls, muffin tins, colored sugar, etc. Ask the children for a suggestion of what you will pretend to bake. Stir up a batch of cookies or a cake, pop it in the pretend oven, and while it bakes, read stories. After storytime, share the pretend (or real!) treats.

Rest Activities

Song

Treats For Our Friends

(Sung to the tune: "Here We Go 'Round the Mulberry Bush")

This is the way we make the fudge,
Make the fudge, make the fudge.
This is the way we make the fudge,
A treat for our friends.
(Substitute other treats such as: pie, bread, rolls, soup…)

Action Rhyme

Baking Cookies

Eggs, butter, sugar, salt,
(Pretend to put each item in the bowl.)
Cocoa powder, vanilla, malt, *(Add each item.)*
Nuts and raisins, in they go. *(Add each item.)*
Mixing up the cookie dough. *(Pretend to stir.)*
Drop by spoonfuls, lick the bowl.
(Pretend to spoon out dough.)
Bake them. Eat them. Good as gold!
(Rub tummy.)

Fingerplay

Making Popcorn Balls

First you pop the corn, Pop, pop, pop,
(Open and close hands quickly.)
Oops, too much. Stop, stop, stop.
(Clap three times.)
Pour the syrup on, Drip, drip, drip.
(Pretend to pour.)
Lick a little taste from your fingertip.
(Lick finger.)
Stir it with a spoon, shape it in a ball.
(Pretend to stir, form a ball with hands.)
Make a dozen popcorn balls. Eat them all!
(Pretend to eat.)

Books to Share

Beil, Karen Magnuson. *A Cake All for Me.* Holiday House, 1998. Using the themes and rhythms of traditional nursery rhymes, gives directions for baking and sharing a cake including "nine, ten, eggs from the hen" and "fifteen, sixteen, a big bowl for mixing."

Rylant, Cynthia. *The Cookie-store Cat.* Blue Sky Press, 1999. A happy cat lives a wonderful life in the back of a cookie store, where the bakers take loving care of him and he receives special visitors.

Schwartz, Ellen. *Mr. Belinsky's Bagels.* Charlesbridge, 1998. When Mr. Belinsky the bagel maker tries his hand at making fancy cookies and cakes, his loyal customers are disappointed, until he returns to creating his specialty.

Soto, Gary. *Too Many Tamales.* Putnam, 1992. Maria tries on her mother's wedding ring while making tamales for a Christmas family get together, but panic ensues when hours later, she realizes the ring is missing.

Chef Recipe Holder

After storytime, help children make these recipe holders (the pocket may be used to hold recipe cards). Suggest the children give theirs as a gift.

glue here

Directions

You will need one whole paper plate and one half paper plate per child. Copy the chef pattern and cut out. Cut a paper plate in half. Place glue on the half paper plate along the outer edge, and glue it to the whole paper plate. At storytime, the children may color the chef, then paste it to the inside edge of the half paper plate, as shown.

 This craft takes 10 minutes to complete.

Candles and Bells

Before Sharing Books

Bring an assortment of candles and bells to display. You may include menorah candles, advent candles, Kwanzaa candles, etc. Talk about the variety of holiday traditions the children observe. Discuss the kinds of bells people hear at holiday time, including doorbells when visitors come, telephones, church bells and bell choirs playing holiday music.

Rest Activities

Songs

Jingle Bells (*Traditional*)
Dashing through the snow,
In a one-horse open sleigh.
O'er the hills we go,
Laughing all the way.
Bells on bobtail ring,
Making spirits bright.
What fun it is to ride and sing,
A sleighing song tonight.

Jingle bells, jingle bells,…

I Have a Little Dreidel (*Traditional*)
I have a little dreidel,
I made it out of clay,
And when it's dry and ready,
Then dreidel I shall play.

Oh dreidel, dreidel, dreidel,
I made it out of clay,
Oh dreidel, dreidel, dreidel,
Now dreidel I shall play.

It has a lovely body,
With leg so short and thin,
And when it gets all tired,
It drops and then I win!

Oh dreidel, dreidel, dreidel,
With leg so short and thin,
Oh dreidel, dreidel, dreidel,
It drops and then I win!

Rhyme

Jack Be Nimble (*Traditional*)
Jack be nimble. Jack be quick.
Jack jump over the candlestick.

Fingerplay

Doorbell Surprise
(*Interlace fingers. Make fist with thumbs on the outside. The fist is your house, and thumbs are the doors. Move thumbs to open doors. Open fist to reveal interlaced fingers, which are the people who came to sing.*)

This is the door on my house.
I heard the doorbell ring.
I opened the door, and what a surprise.
The people began to sing.

Books to Share

Dixon, Ann. *Merry Birthday, Nora Noel.* Eerdmans, 1996. Nora Noel's father lights the advent candles, and tells her the story of how the whole family looked forward to her arrival and how they celebrated her birth as their own Christmas baby.

Kimmel, Eric A. *When Mindy Saved Hanukkah.* Scholastic, 1998. A tiny Jewish family living behind the wall of a synagogue must battle a frightening cat if they want candles for their Hanukkah menorah.

Medearis, Angela Shelf. *Seven Spools of Thread: A Kwanzaa Story.* A. Whitman, 2000. When they are given the seemingly impossible task of turning thread into gold, the seven Ashanti brothers put aside their differences, learn to get along and embody the principles of Kwanzaa.

Rosen, Michael J. *Our Eight Nights of Hanukkah.* Holiday House, 2000. A child describes how one family celebrates Hanukkah, including polishing the silver menorah, lighting the candles, having a special family dinner and sharing gifts.

Spinelli, Eileen. *Coming Through the Blizzard.* Simon & Schuster Books for Young Readers, 1999. The Minister lit the candles and waited to see if anyone would come to the Christmas Eve service, through the blizzard.

Stained Glass Bell

Children can make these bells for use as an ornament or a gift!

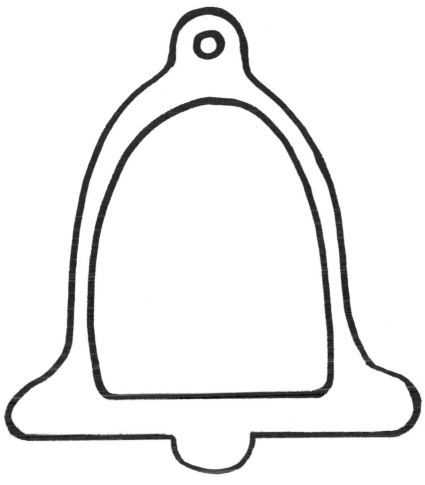

Directions

Copy the pattern on colored paper and cut out to make a frame. Punch a hole in the top using a paper punch. Cut an 8" piece of yarn or string, put it through the hole and tie it to form a hanger. Copy the pattern on tissue paper and cut out, but do not cut out the center. Paste the tissue paper behind the frame. At storytime, the children may paste tiny bits of colored tissue paper on the bell in layers, creating a stained glass look. A glue stick works well for this.

 This craft takes 5 minutes to complete.

Gifts

Before Sharing Books

Collect boxes with lids that can be removed. Place a variety of gift-like things in the boxes. Wrap them in colorful paper, which may include holiday paper and birthday paper. One at a time, open the boxes and show the gifts to the children. These may include a drawing from a child, a photograph, an old teddy bear, a new pair of socks, etc. Talk about the thought behind each gift, and to whom they would like to give such a gift.

Rest Activities

Songs

Three Little Presents

(Sung to the tune: "10 Little Indians")

One little, two little, three little presents,
Opening them will be so pleasant.
Two are for me and one of them isn't,
Happy, happy day.

Teapots and Jacks-in-the-box are just a couple of traditional gifts that are given. You may use the following song and rhyme to start discussions about some of the children's favorite gifts they have received.

I'm a Little Teapot *(Traditional)*

I'm a little teapot, short and stout.
Here is my handle, here is my spout.
When I get all steamed up, here me shout.
Tip me over and pour me out.

Action Rhymes

Jack-in-the-box *(Traditional)*

Jack-in-the-box,
Sit so still. *(Crouch.)*
Won't you come out?
YES, I will!!! *(Jump up.)*

What Is In the Box?

I wonder what's in that great big box.
(Draw a large square with fingers.)
Could it be a big ball?
(Stretch arms out, forming a large circle.)
Could it be a teddy bear?
(Pretend to hug a teddy bear.)
Or a toy car, very small?
(With index finger and thumb pretend to hold toy car.)

Books to Share

Mora, Pat. *A Birthday Basket for Tia.* Macmillan, 1992. With the help and interference of her cat Chica, Cecilia prepares a surprise gift for her great-aunt's ninetieth birthday.

Shepard, Aaron. *The Baker's Dozen: A Saint Nicholas Tale.* Atheneum Books for Young Readers, 1995. A baker in colonial New York learns the importance of generosity from an old woman who visits his shop on St. Nicholas Day.

Sun, Chyng-Feng. *Mama Bear.* Houghton Mifflin, 1994. When Mei-Mei fails in her attempt to earn money through a cookie sale for the expensive toy bear she wants for Christmas, her mother helps her see a special gift she has had all along.

Wells, Rosemary. *Morris's Disappearing Bag.* Viking, 1999. Everyone in Morris' family is pleased with his Christmas present except Morris.

Decorate a Gift

Show children some basic gift decorating techniques, then make this craft.

Directions

Copy the bow and tag patterns and cut out. At story-time, give each child a large unlined index card. Let the children decorate their cards using rubber stamps or stickers. You may choose holiday shapes, flowers, teddy bears or any other design for this craft. The children may then color and paste on the bow and tag, using a glue stick.

 This craft takes 10 minutes to complete.

Arctic & Antarctic Animals

Before Sharing Books

Have all the children put on their pretend mittens, boots and hats. Walk in place as you crunch the snow, slip on the ice, climb up an iceberg. Have everyone sit on the pretend iceberg and look out for animals. Ask the children what animals they might see in this very cold place.

Rest Activities

Song

The Penguin Song

(Sung to the tune: "The Farmer in the Dell")

The penguin wears a suit.
The penguin wears a suit.
Did you ever wonder why,
The penguin wears a suit?

He's dressed up for the dance.
He's dressed up for the dance.
Now you know just why,
The penguin wears a suit!

Action Rhymes

The Walrus

One walrus waddled on the wide, white ice.
(Walk in place with large steps.)
Wiggled his whiskers once or twice.
(Place fingers by chin and wiggle them.)
He waved to a whale with his long white tusks.
(Place index fingers by chin.)
Then he waddled back home, along about dusk.
(Walk in place again.)

Arctic Animals

Salmon swim. *(Move hands like a fish.)*
Lemmings creep. *(Fingers walk up arm.)*
Wolves howl. *(Tip head and howl.)*
Sled dogs sleep. *(Rest chin on hands.)*
Ravens fly. *(Stretch arms out like wings.)*
Whales sing.
(Use hand to pantomime a whale swimming.)
Polar bears eat 'most anything!
(Place hands by mouth and pretend to eat.)

Books to Share

Brooks, Erik. *The Practically Perfect Pajamas.* Winslow Press, 2000. Percy gives up his beloved footed pajamas after the other polar bears tease him about them, but then he realizes how useful they were.

De Beer, Hans. *Little Polar Bear and the Husky Pup.* North-South Books, 1999. Lars the Little Polar Bear rescues a stranded husky puppy and helps her find food and her mother.

Joosse, Barbara. *Mama, Do You Love Me?* Chronicle Books, 1991. A child living in the Arctic learns that a mother's love is unconditional.

Kern, Noris. I *Love You With All My Heart.* Chronicle Books, 1998. Polo the polar bear asks his mother how she loves him, and she explains that she loves him with her eyes, her nose, her paws, and all her heart.

Moss, Miriam. *Arctic Song.* BridgeWater Books, 1999. Bewitched by the raven's description of whale song, two polar bear cubs go in search of the whales, encountering caribou, a walrus, and other animals on the way. Includes a factual page about life in the Arctic.

Waddell, Martin. *Little Mo.* Candlewick Press, 1993. The Big Ones try to help a young polar bear learn how to glide on the ice, but she gets bumped so much that she decides it isn't any fun—until she spends time learning on her own.

Wood, Audrey. *Little Penguin's Tale.* Harcourt Brace Jovanovich, 1989. Searching for fun in his snowy polar world, Little Penguin dances with the gooney birds, cavorts at the Walrus Polar Club, and narrowly escapes being caten by a whale.

Walrus

Talk about the walrus' habitat and behavior while children make this take-along.

Directions
Copy the pattern on colored paper and cut out. At storytime, let the children glue the shapes together using a glue stick to make the walrus. Optional: let the children glue on snips of yarn for the walrus' whiskers.

 This craft takes 10 minutes to complete.

Playing in the Snow

Before Sharing Books

Have the children mime with you rolling a snowball about baseball size. Toss it in the air and catch it. Roll it bigger, to basketball size. Ask the children, "Is it heavy?" Now roll it as big as your arms can reach around. Ask the children, "Is it too heavy to lift?" Roll it down a hill. Watch it go faster and faster. When it stops at the bottom of the hill, have everyone sit down for stories.

Rest Activities

Song

Snow Song
(Sung to the tune: "Are You Sleeping")

Snow is falling. Snow is falling.
Soft and white. Soft and white.
Let's go out and play. Let's go out and play.
Snowball fight. Snowball fight.

Action Rhyme

It's Snowing

It's snowing, *(Fingers make snowflakes falling.)*
Out I go. *(March in place.)*
I make a snow angel. *(Spread arms out to sides.)*
I wave hello. *(Wave.)*
My friend throws a snowball.
I catch it like this. *(Pretend to catch it.)*
I throw one back even bigger than his.
(Pretend to throw.)
My nose is cold. *(Touch nose.)*

Time to go. *(Wave good-bye.)*
Back in the house,
For some warm cocoa.
(Pretend to sip a cup of cocoa.)

Fingerplay

Mouse In the Snow

A little white mouse creeps out in the snow.
(Fingers walk up arm.)
Leaving tiny footprints wherever he goes.
(Thumb and index finger almost touch.)
Owl can't see him, the little mouse knows.
(Fingers form circles. Place them over the eyes.)
So he plays all day long, then home he goes.
(Walk fingers up the arm, then quickly put arms behind back.)

Books to Share

Brennan, Linda Crotta. *Flannel Kisses.* Houghton Mifflin, 1997. Rhyming text describes a winter day spent playing in the snow.

Brown, Margaret Wise. *Animals in the Snow.* Hyperion Books for Children, 1995. When snow falls, the animals stay home; when it stops, they come out to play; and when it melts, it is spring!

Chapman, Cheryl. *Snow On Snow On Snow.* Dial Books for Young Readers, 1994. The author uses repetitive wordplay to tell the story of a boy who loses and then recovers his dog while sledding in the snow.

Ehlert, Lois. *Snowballs.* Harcourt Brace, 1995. Some children create a family out of snow. Includes labeled

pictures of all the items they use, as well as information about how snow is formed.

George, Lindsay Barrett. *In the Snow: Who's Been Here?* Greenwillow Books, 1995. Two children on their way to go sledding see evidence of a variety of animal life.

Kirk, Daniel. *The Snow Family.* Hyperion Books for Children, 2000. A young boy decides to build a snow family to take care of his snowboy the way his parents take care of him.

Neitzel, Shirley. *The Jacket I Wear In the Snow.* Greenwillow Books, 1989. A young girl names all the clothes that she must wear to play in the snow.

Snow Scene

You may want to display a photo of what a snow-covered tree looks like before children make this craft.

Directions

Provide a blue paper plate for each child. Cut out one tree pattern for each child from brown paper. Allow the children to glue the tree on the paper plate, then glue on torn pieces of cotton balls to create a snow scene.

 This craft takes 10 minutes to complete.

Chinese New Year

Before Sharing Books

Show the children a bowl of oranges and tangerines. Tell them that it is good luck to display these fruits for Chinese New Year. Oranges mean you hope to receive money, and tangerines mean you hope to receive good luck. If possible, show a red gift envelope called a "lai see." Tell the children that gifts of money are given to children in these envelopes on Chinese New Year.

Rest Activities

Song

Chinese New Year's Day Parade

(Sung to the tune: "The Bear Went Over the Mountain")
I see a lion,
I see a lion,
I see a lion,
In the New Year's Day Parade.

The New Year's Day Parade.
The New Year's Day Parade.

I see a lion,
I see a lion,
I see a lion,
in the New Year's Day Parade.
(Repeat, substituting "dragon" for "lion.")

Action Rhyme

Getting Ready for Chinese New Year

Sweep away the bad luck,
(Move arms as if sweeping.)
Wipe away the dust.
(Wave hand in air.)
Put on your new shoes,
Everybody must.
(Pretend to put on shoes.)
We're ready for the New Year.
Everybody smile.
(Place hands by face and smile.)
Good luck is coming,
To stay for a while.*(Put arm around person next to you.)*

Books to Share

Chinn, Karen. ***Sam and the Lucky Money.*** Lee & Low Books, 1995. Sam must decide how to spend the lucky money he's received for Chinese New Year.

Compestine, Ying Chang. ***The Runaway Rice Cake.*** Simon & Schuster Books for Young Readers, 2001. After chasing the special rice cake, Nian Gao, that their mother has made to celebrate the Chinese New Year, three poor brothers share it with an elderly woman and have their generosity richly rewarded.

Hoyt-Goldsmith, Diane. ***Celebrating Chinese New Year.*** Holiday House, 1998. Depicts a San Francisco boy

and his family preparing for and enjoying their celebration of the Chinese New Year, their most important holiday.

Steckman, Elizabeth. ***Silk Peony, Parade Dragon.*** Boyds Mills Press, 1997. How Mrs. Ming's pet dragon, Silk Peony, becomes the official parade dragon of China.

Young, Ed. ***The Lost Horse: A Chinese Folktale.*** Silver Whistle/Harcourt Brace, 1998. A retelling of the tale about a Chinese man who owned a marvelous horse and who believed that things were not always as bad, or as good, as they might seem.

Good Luck Dragon Card

After children learn about Chinese New Year, they will enjoy having their own "good luck" dragon to take home with them.

Directions

Cut a 6" square of red paper for each child. Copy the dragon pattern and cut out one per child. Allow the children to glue the dragon on the red paper using a glue stick. The children may color the dragon also, if they wish. Tell them red is the color of good luck, and that dragons are good luck also. Suggest that they hang their Good Luck Dragon in their home for a holiday decoration.

 This craft takes 5 minutes to complete.

Quilts and Blankets

Before Sharing Books

Show several full-size or baby-size quilts. Tell about how and when each quilt was made. Show some cut quilt pieces and show how they fit together to form a pattern. Show the top, fluffy middle and bottom fabric of a quilt. Tell the children that the three parts of a quilt are what make it fluffy.

Rest Activities

Action Rhymes

The Blanket

One soft blanket on my bed,
(*Pull blanket up to chin.*)
Two little pillows for my head,
(*Rest head on hands.*)
Three gentle kisses for a restful night,
(*Blow three kisses.*)
Four quick hugs, then off goes the light.
(*Cross arms and squeeze, then pretend to switch off light.*)

This Little Boy (Adapted traditional)
(*Pantomime actions as they are mentioned in the rhyme.*)

This little boy all ready for bed.
Down on the pillow he lays his head.
Wraps himself in his blankets tight.
And this is the way he sleeps all night.

Morning comes. He opens his eyes.
Back with a toss his blankets fly.
Up he jumps! Is dressed and away.
Ready to work and play all day.

Fingerplay

Grandma's Quilt

Grandma cuts bits of green, blue and white.
(*Move fingers like scissors.*)
She moves them around until they look just right.
(*Cross hands, then cross back.*)
While she stitches the pieces together she smiles.
(*One hand mimes stitching on palm of other hand.*)
When her fingers get tired she rests for a while.
(*Fold hands in lap.*)
Stitch and stitch the quilt, then sip a cup of tea.
(*Pretend to stitch, then pretend to hold teacup to lips.*)
I hope when it's finished, she will give it to me.
(*Point to self.*)

Books to Share

Apple, Margot. *Blanket.* Houghton Mifflin, 1990. When Blanket is hung on the clothesline overnight to dry, the rest of the clothes, the dog, the cat, and the wind work together to get it safely inside to its owner.

Geras, Adèle. *From Lullaby to Lullaby.* Simon & Schuster, 1997. A lullaby in which a parent, while knitting a blanket for a child, describes the dreams of each of the objects pictured in the blanket.

Gilman, Phoebe. *Something from Nothing.* Scholastic, 1993. In this retelling of a traditional Jewish folktale, Joseph's baby blanket is transformed into ever-smaller items as he grows until there is nothing left—but then Joseph has an idea.

Henkes, Kevin. *Owen.* Greenwillow Books, 1993. Owen's parents try to get him to give up his favorite blanket before he starts school, but when their efforts fail, they come up with a solution that makes everyone happy.

Kuskin, Karla. *Patchwork Island.* HarperCollins, 1994. A mother making a quilt for her child stitches the varied topography of their beautiful island into her patchwork pattern.

Stevens, Janet. *Coyote Steals the Blanket: A Ute Tale.* Holiday House, 1993. Coyote receives his comeuppance when he tries to take something that does not belong to him.

Warner, Sunny. *The Moon Quilt.* Houghton Mifflin, 2001. With her cat in her lap, an old woman makes a quilt, stitching into it the experiences and objects of her life.

Baby in a Blanket

Talking and reading about quilts will put children in the mood for this snuggly craft.

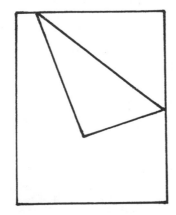

Directions

Fold a 9" x 6" piece of colored paper in half to 4½" x 6". Fold back a corner as shown in the illustration at right. Copy the patterns and cut out. Allow the children to glue along two edges of the blanket as shown using a glue stick. Let them glue the sleeping baby back to back with the awake baby. Put the baby in the blanket, sleepy side out. When he wakes up, turn him around so the awake baby shows.

 This craft takes 10 minutes to complete.

Red, Red, Red

Before Sharing Books

Display a variety of red objects, such as apples, shoes, toys, Valentine candy boxes, clothing, a red wagon or red flowers. Ask the children what is the same about these objects. Are they the same size? Can you eat all of them? Can you play with all of them? Are they the same color?

Rest Activities

Song

Red Song

(Sung to the tune: "Mary Had a Little Lamb")

I can think of something red,
Something red, something red.
I can think of something red,
Catsup is red.

(Substitute other "red" words in the last line, such as Valentines, ladybugs, fire trucks....)

Action Rhyme

Apple Tree (Traditional)

Way up high in the apple tree,
(Stretch arms overhead.)
Two red apples were looking at me.
(Make circles with fingers, place in front of eyes.)
So I shook and I shook and I shook that tree,
(Pretend to grab tree trunk and shake it.)

Until those red apples came down to me.
(Hit floor with hands.)
Good! *(Pretend to take a bite.)*

Fingerplay

Four Red Clowns

Four red clowns stand up tall.
1, 2, 3, 4.
(Hold fingers up as you count.)
Oops! Oops! Down they fall.
4, 3, 2, 1.
(Curl fingers into fist as you count down.)

Books to Share

Blackstone, Stella. *Can You See the Red Balloon?* Orchard Books, 1998. The reader is asked to pick out objects of different colors in each picture, plus the black-and-white cow that appears on every page.

Brothers Grimm; illustrated by Lisbeth Zwerger; translated by Elizabeth D. Crawford. *Little Red Cap.* North-South Books, 1995. A little girl meets a hungry wolf in the forest while on her way to visit her sick grandmother.

Climo, Shirley. T*he Little Red Ant and the Great Big Crumb: A Mexican Fable.* Clarion Books, 1995. A small red ant finds a crumb in a Mexican cornfield, but she is afraid that she lacks the strength to move it herself and goes off to find an animal that can.

Compton, Joanne. *Ashpet: An Appalachian Tale.* Holiday House, 1994. In this Appalachian variant of the Cinderella tale, old Granny helps Ashpet attend the church picnic where she charms Doc Ellison's son but loses one of her fancy red shoes.

Garner, Alan. *Little Red Hen.* DK Pub., 1997. A retelling of the story of a resourceful hen that not only makes her own food and eats it herself, but manages to outwit a hungry fox as well.

Kleven, Elisa. *The Lion and the Little Red Bird.* Dutton Children's Books, 1992. A little bird discovers why the lion's tail changes color each day.

Seeing Red

Explain to the children how colored lenses cause everything they see through them to appear in that color.

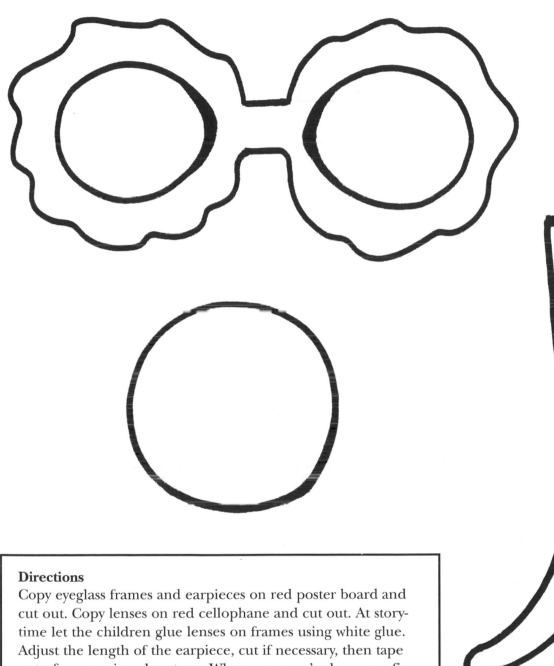

Directions

Copy eyeglass frames and earpieces on red poster board and cut out. Copy lenses on red cellophane and cut out. At story-time let the children glue lenses on frames using white glue. Adjust the length of the earpiece, cut if necessary, then tape onto frames using clear tape. When everyone's glasses are finished, put on a pair of glasses and say, "I see red Michael, red Sarah, red book, red chair..." List other things that are visible. Ask the children if they see a red hand, a red girl, a red boy, etc. This craft takes 10 minutes to complete. Volunteers are helpful in assembling the glasses. The Seeing Red activity takes an additional 5 minutes.

 This craft takes 10 minutes to complete.

Valentine's Day

Before Sharing Books

With your finger, draw a circle in the air. Now draw a square in the air. Now draw a pocket, round or square, on your shirt or pants. Reach inside this pocket and pull out a Valentine. Draw a heart shape in the air. Tell the children this Valentine is just for them.

Rest Activities

Song

Valentine Song

(Sung to the tune: "Happy Birthday")

Happy Valentine's Day,
I just wanted to say,
I'm glad you are my friend.
Let's go out and play!

Action Rhyme

I Like You

I like ice cream.
(Lick a cone.)
I like cake.
(Bring fork to mouth and eat a bite.)
I like the sounds,
That kittens make.
(Pet a kitten.)
I like kites.
(Hold kite string.)
In the sky so blue,
And most of all,
I like you.
(Point to self, then point to a friend.)

Clapping Rhyme

Be My Valentine

(Practice this clapping sequence: Clap hands, then pat lap three times. Add the words, beginning slowly. Do it several more times, each time a little faster.)

Will you be, be, be,
My Valentine, tine, tine,
That will be, be, be,
Just fine, fine, fine!

Books to Share

Carrick, Carol. *Valentine.* Clarion Books, 1995. While waiting for her mother to come home from work on Valentine's Day, Heather helps her grandmother rescue a newborn lamb and bake a special cookie.

Hoban, Lillian. *Silly Tilly's Valentine.* HarperCollins Publishers, 1998. Mr. Bunny reminds her that the day is special, but while trying to recall why, Silly Tilly, the forgetful mole, gets distracted by the snow.

Roberts, Bethany. *Valentine Mice!* Clarion Books, 1997. An energetic group of mice delivers Valentines to the other animals.

Shannon, George. *Heart to Heart.* Houghton Mifflin, 1995. Upset that he has forgotten a Valentine for his friend Mole, Squirrel starts to make a fancy card but discovers a better gift.

Felt Heart Necklace

Children will want to wear this necklace or give it to someone special.

Directions

Cut a 24" piece of yarn or nylon chord for each child.
Cut out one felt heart, using pattern, for each child.
Hot glue the yarn in place as shown in the illustration.
At storytime, let each child glue a ribbon rose on the
felt heart using tacky craft glue.

 This craft takes 5 minutes to complete.

The Post Office

Before Sharing Books

Display postcards from your vacation or a stamp collection. Show an envelope and indicate where the stamp is placed for mailing. Ask if anyone knows what the building is called where you take your letters so they will be delivered to faraway places. Talk about how letters get to their destinations, such as by plane, truck or boat. Ask the children who brings the mail to their house.

Rest Activities

Action Rhyme

Mailing a Letter

Mamma and I went for a walk, *(Walk in place.)*
To mail a letter to Gran.
She lifted me up, *(Stand on toes.)*
I dropped it in *(Push letter in.)*
Then we walked home again. *(Walk in place.)*

Clapping Rhyme

How Many Letters Today?

(Clap even rhythm on lap while reciting this rhyme.)

My Daddy lets me put on the stamps,
Before he mails his letters.
How many letters today, Daddy?
The more you have, the better.
Three letters today, Daddy?
1, 2, 3.
If you need help tomorrow, Daddy,
Just ask me!

Game

Guessing Game

There was something special in the mail today.
Can you guess what it might be?
(Show a picture of something children enjoy, such as puppies, cars, toys, food…)
No, not a _____
It was a birthday card for me!
(Show a birthday card.)

Books to Share

Boelts, Maribeth. *Grace and Joe.* A. Whitman, 1994. A preschooler finds a friend in her neighborhood mail carrier.

Bridwell, Norman. *Clifford's First Valentine's Day.* Scholastic, 1997. Emily Elizabeth tells about Clifford's first Valentine's Day when he was still a tiny puppy. Clifford goes to the post office with Emily Elizabeth to mail valentines and gets lost in the carts full of letters.

Flanagan, Alice K. *Here Comes Mr. Eventoff with the Mail!* Children's Press, 1998. Follows a letter carrier for a day at his job from the time he arrives at the post office to pick up and sort the mail until the last item is delivered.

Hobbie, Holly. *Toot and Puddle.* Little, Brown, 1997. Toot and Puddle are best friends with very different interests, so as Toot spends the year traveling around the world, Puddle enjoys receiving his postcards.

Olson, Mary W. *Nice Try, Tooth Fairy.* Simon & Schuster Books for Young Readers, 1999. Hoping to get back her lost tooth, Emma writes a series of letters to the Tooth Fairy, but when the wrong teeth keep getting returned the mistakes create complications.

Scott, Ann Herbert. *Hi!* Philomel Books, 1994. While waiting in line with her mother at the post office, Margarita greets the patrons who come in carrying different types of mail.

Postcard for the Mail Carrier

Children love to thank people in public service. Help them make this thank you card, and tell them they can give it to their mail carrier.

Dear Mail Carrier,

Thank you for bringing my mail.

Directions
Copy the pattern on index paper and cut out. Let the children draw a picture on the blank side of the postcard.

 This craft takes 5 minutes to complete.

I Love My Friends

Before Sharing Books

Show a photo of one of your friends. Tell the children the name of your friend, and something the two of you enjoy doing together. Ask the children to raise their hand if they have a friend. List some activities and ask them to raise their hand if they enjoy doing that activity with their friend.

Rest Activities

Action Story

My Friend

(Lead the children in acting out the following.)

My friend and I like many things.
We like to hop.
We like to run.
We like to climb trees and while we are up there,
We like to look far, far away.
Then we climb down.
After playing, we like to sit and listen to stories.

Clapping Rhyme

Friendship Clapping Rhyme

(Sung to the tune: "A Sailor Went to Sea")

(Have children face their parent or another child. Clap in this sequence: clap their hands, cross hands and clap their partner's hand, clap their hands, cross opposite hand and clap their partner's hand, clap their hands, clap both hands of their partner three times. Start slowly, then try it faster. When they have the clapping sequence, add the words.)

My best friends said to me, me, me,
I'll call you up at three, three, three.
A movie we will see, see, see,
What fun for you and me, me, me.

Fingerplays

The House On My Block

There's a house on my block, not far away.
(Make a fist.)
Whenever I knock, *(Knock on fist with other fist.)*
My friends come out to play. *(Open hand.)*
1, 2, 3, 4, 5! *(Count fingers.)*

Rainy Day Play

Two friends went out to play, *(Hold up two fingers.)*
On a lovely morning.
The clouds rolled in, *(Roll hands.)*
The rain began, *(Wiggle fingers.)*
And soon it was pouring! *(Clap on lap.)*
The friends ran home,
With a wave and a shout, *(Wave.)*
And when the rain stopped, *(Hands behind back.)*
They came back out. *(Hold up two fingers again.)*

Books to Share

Freymann, Saxton. ***One Lonely Seahorse.*** Arthur A. Levine Books, 2000. One lonely sea horse learns that she has a lot of friends—friends she can really "count" on.

Horstman, Lisa. ***Fast Friends: A Tail and Tongue Tale.*** Knopf: Distributed by Random House, 1994. A cow and a chameleon move to the big city and become roommates until their considerable differences threaten to ruin their friendship.

Kilborne, Sarah S. ***Peach & Blue.*** Knopf: Distributed by Random House, 1994. A frog helps a peach see the world and the peach shows the frog sights he has never seen before.

Lewis, Kim. ***Friends.*** Candlewick Press, 1997. While searching for eggs on the farm, Sam and Alice discover that they can be better friends when they cooperate with each other.

Munson, Derek. ***Enemy Pie.*** Chronicle Books, 2000. Hoping that the enemy pie which his father makes will help him get rid of his enemy, a little boy finds that instead it helps make a new friend.

Spoon Friend

Some of the children may have imaginary friends. Consider talking about those friends before making this craft.

Directions
Provide a plastic spoon, two small round stickers, and a pipe cleaner for each child. Have felt pens available for drawing the mouth. *Optional:* provide scraps of yarn, fabric, felt and tacky glue for creating clothing and hair.

Let the children wrap the pipe cleaner around the spoon to create arms. Let them place the round stickers on the spoon for eyes, and draw a mouth with the felt pen.

This craft takes 5 minutes to complete when not using fabric and glue. It takes 10 to 15 minutes to complete when using fabric and glue.

 This craft takes 5 minutes to complete.

Green

Before Sharing Books

Tell the children you want to play a game called "I Am Thinking of Something Green." Give hints to the children and let them guess what you are thinking of. Some suggested objects for this game are: broccoli, inchworm, tree, green eyes, turtle, frog.... Some suggested hints are: "it is smaller than my fist," "it is something that moves," "it is something you can eat," and "it is something that makes a noise."

Rest Activities

Song

Do You Know What's Green?

(Sung to the tune: "Row, Row, Row Your Boat")

Do, do, do you know,
Do you know what's green?
Trees and grass and turtles and beans.
Lots of things are green.

Action Rhymes

I Like Green

I climb green trees.

(Hand over hand.)
I eat green peas.
(Pretend to bring spoon to mouth.)
I catch green frogs.
(Quickly grab pretend frog with both hands.)
That hop on logs.
I watch green worms.
(Wiggle finger.)
That wiggle and squirm.

I like green, it's true.
(Point to self.)
How about you?
(Point to somebody else.)

When I Wear My Green Hat

When I wear my green hat,
(Pretend to put a hat on your head.)
I have a good day.
(Smile and point to face.)
My friends and I,
(Pretend to point to two friends, then self.)
Have fun at play.
(Skip in place.)
When I wear my green shirt,
(Point to shirt.)
It makes me smile.
(Smile and point to face.)
I climb a tall tree,
(Hand over hand.)
And I can see for miles.
(Place hand over eyebrows, pretend to look far away.)

Books to Share

Anholt, Catherine. *A Kiss Like This.* Barron's Educational Series, 1997. Little Cub enjoys the kisses of Big Golden Lion, as well as those of the other animals, until Mean Green Hungry Crocodile tries to kiss him.

Arnold, Tedd. *Green Wilma.* Dial Books for Young Readers, 1993. Waking up with a frog-like appearance, Wilma proves disruptive at school as she searches for some tasty flies.

Emberley, Ed. *Go Away, Big Green Monster.* Little, Brown, 1992. Die-cut pages through which bits of a monster are revealed are designed to help a child control nighttime fears of monsters.

McCourt, Lisa. *I Love You, Stinky Face.* Troll, 1997. A mother and child discuss how the mother's love would remain constant even if her child were a stinky skunk, scary ape, or bug-eating green alien.

Winne, Joanne. *Green In My World.* Children's Press, 2000. A simple story highlights such green things as green eyes, a green soccer uniform, and salad.

Woolfitt, Gabrielle. *Green.* Carolrhoda Books, 1992. Text and photographs describe common things that are green, including trees, fruit, and parrots.

Green Bookworm

Make this happy bookworm at the end of your green storytime!

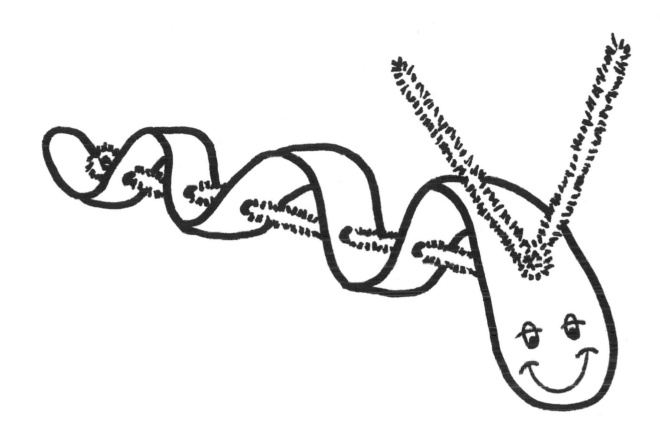

Directions

Cut a 12" pipe cleaner in to two pieces, 8" and 4". Form a loop in one end of the 8" pipe cleaner. Put the 4" pipe cleaner through the loop and twist. This will become the bookworm's feelers.

Cut a 12" x 1½" strip of green construction paper and round the ends. Use a paper punch to make six holes evenly spaced along the center of the paper strip. Repeat these steps for each child.

At storytime, the children can thread the pipe cleaner through the holes, going in one hole, then out the next, etc., and then slide the paper toward the feelers, making the worm curved. Curl the end of the pipe cleaner to form a tail, and to prevent the pipe cleaner from going through the last hole.

Allow the children to draw a face on their bookworm with crayons or markers.

 This craft takes 5 minutes to complete.

St. Patrick's Day

Before Sharing Books

Welcome the children to the St. Patrick's Day Celebration. Tell them that many people from Ireland celebrate this day, and many others act as if they are Irish for one day to join in the fun. Tell the children that in some cities there will be a parade, people wear green clothes or shamrocks and listen to Irish music. Play a recording of Irish folk music, then begin your stories.

Rest Activities

Song

Wearing Green

(Sung to the tune: "A Hunting We Will Go")

I wore green socks today.
I wore green socks today.
I'm wearing green today,
This is St. Patrick's Day.
(Substitute other items such as: green shirt, green button, green bow, green pants, green shoes…)

Action Rhyme

The Little Man

I met a little man,
(Hold hand out at waist high.)
With whiskers on his chin.
(Stroke chin.)
I said, "Good day to you, sir."
(Wave.)
He began to grin.
(Point to face.)
"You didn't try to catch me,"
(Shake finger.)

He said with a wink.
(Point to eye.)
Then he gave me a penny for luck.
(Hold out hand palm up.)
He was a leprechaun, I think.
(Nod head.)

Poem

Shamrock

How many leaves on a shamrock?
One, two, three.
One for you, one for you,
And one for me.

Books to Share

Bateman, Teresa. **Leprechaun Gold.** Holiday House, 1998. When Donald O'Dell saves the life of a leprechaun but refuses his offer of gold, he finds his good deed rewarded in an unexpected fashion.

Dillon, Jana. **Lucky O'Leprechaun.** Pelican Pub., 1998. On St. Patrick's Day eve, Meghan and Sean manage to capture a sly leprechaun.

Korman, Justine. **The Luckiest Leprechaun.** Troll/BridgeWater Books, 2000. When a leprechaun reluctantly lets a dog befriend him, he finds out what it's like to care about someone.

Robertson, Ivan. **Jack and the Leprechaun.** Random House, 2000. Jack the mouse goes to visit his cousin in Ireland on St. Patrick's Day, and spends the day trying to catch a leprechaun.

Potato Puppet

Explain the connection between Ireland and potatoes before making this puppet.

Directions

Cut two potatoes, one with a face and one without, using the pattern. From green paper, cut four shamrocks, using the pattern. Cut four 2" lengths of green wrapping ribbon. Before storytime, glue shamrocks to the ribbons and glue ribbons to one potato as shown in the illustration, making arms and legs. At storytime let the children glue the second potato on top of the first, leaving the bottom open between small dots. Slide it over the child's hand.

 This craft takes 5 minutes to complete.

Windy Day

Before Sharing Books

Have the children make the sound of a gentle breeze, a small wind, and a strong wind. Tell them that wind can be tricky sometimes, and ask them to tell some tricks that wind might play, such as messing up your hair, tugging on your shirt, blowing papers around the neighborhood, or shaking the trees. Tell them that wind can be useful, too. Wind can take up a kite, turn a wind-mill, or turn a pinwheel. Show a pinwheel and blow on it to demonstrate how it works.

Rest Activities

Action Rhyme

Ladybug

A ladybug climbed up a dandelion,
(Fingers walk from shoulder to top of head.)
She got to the top and was feeling fine.
The wind came along and took her for a spin,
(Finger draws loops in the air.)
Then the ladybug climbed up again.
(Fingers walk up head again.)

Action Story

Windy Day

(Pantomime actions as they are mentioned in the rhyme.)

I went out on a windy day.
I put on my cap.
I zipped up my jacket.
I put my tissue in my pocket.
I pulled up my socks.
I tied my shoes.
Then my cap blew off, so I
Ran, and ran, and ran.
I caught my cap at last,
But I DIDN'T put it on again.

Poem

When the Wind Blows Through

My cat stares out the window,
Watching tree limbs shake.
Her tail twitches nervously,
Her whiskers quake.
She doesn't quite know what to do,
When the wind blows through.
When the wind, the sneaky wind,
The gate slapping, chair tipping,
Twig snapping, flag whipping,
Dust stirring, cap stealing,
Give a cat a freaky feeling...
My cat doesn't know quite what to do,
When the wind blows through.

Books to Share

Carlstrom, Nancy White. *How Does the Wind Walk?* Macmillan, 1993. A little boy watches the wind through the four seasons of the year.

Evans, Lezlie. *If I Were the Wind.* Ideals Children's Books, 1997. A mother offers reassurances that no matter what outlandish event were to happen, she would always find a way to take care of her beloved child.

Ginsburg, Mirra. *Asleep, Asleep.* Greenwillow Books, 1992. Everything everywhere is asleep except for the wind and one wakeful child.

Lipson, Michael. *How the Wind Plays.* Hyperion Books for Children, 1994. The wind, in the form of a mischievous child, indulges in such playful antics as shaking tree branches against windows and blowing snow inside.

McKee, David. *Elmer Takes Off.* Lothrop, Lee & Shepard, 1998. On a very, very windy day Elmer, the patchwork elephant, assures all the other animals and birds that nothing could ever blow him away.

White, Linda Arms. *Comes a Wind.* DK Pub., 2000. While visiting their mother's ranch, two brothers who constantly try to best each other swap tall tales about big winds and are surprised by the fiercest wind they have ever seen.

Twirling Toy

Talk about the "helicopter" seed pods that twirl down from maple trees, then make this twirling toy.

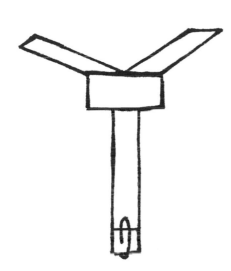

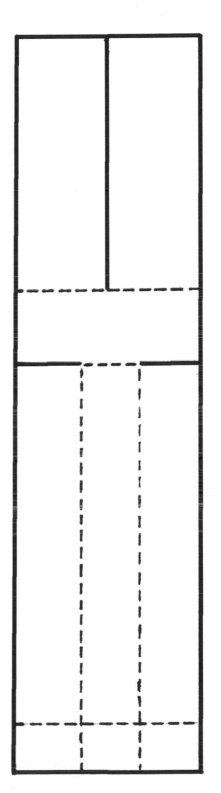

Directions

From colorful wrapping paper or plain-colored copy paper, cut the toy using the pattern. Cut on solid lines. Fold on dotted lines, as illustrated. Repeat these steps for each child. At storytime, show the children how to put a paperclip on the toy. Drop it from shoulder height and watch it twirl like a helicopter.

 This craft takes 5 minutes to complete.

Lions and Lambs

Before Sharing Books

Ask the children to roar like a lion. Then ask them to bah like a lamb. Tell them that in the month of March, the wind can be very strong like a lion, or gentle like a lamb. Now have them make the sounds of a strong wind and a gentle wind. Begin your storytime with books about strong lions, and end with books about gentle lambs.

Rest Activities

Songs

A Lion Likes to Roar

(Sung to the tune: "A Hunting We Will Go")

A lion likes to roar.
A lion likes to roar.
He makes a frightful noise,
And then he roars some more.

Bah, Bah, Black Sheep *(Traditional)*

Bah, bah, black sheep.
Have you any wool?
Yes sir, yes sir,
Three bags full.
One for my master,
One for my dame,
One for the boy,
Who lives down the lane.
Bah, bah, black sheep.
Have you any wool?
Yes sir, yes sir,
Three bags full.

Action Rhyme

The King

I'm a lion, fierce and strong. *(Show muscles.)*
My mane is brown and very long. *(Stroke hair.)*
It sounds loud when I sing.
(Open mouth wide and roar.)
The other animals call me King.
(Put a crown on head.)

Fingerplay

Two Lambs

Over the hill, sunny and green,
Two lambs leap and play.
(Hold up two fingers, one on each hand.)
Where will they go, what will they see,
And what will they do today?
The first one chases a butterfly,
As it follows the little stream.
(Put one hand behind back.)
The last one curls up in the shade,
(Curl finger into fist.)
And dreams, and dreams, and dreams.
(Lay face on hands as if sleeping.)

Books to Share

Gliori, Debi. *A Lion at Bedtime.* Barron's, 1994. Ben is frightened by a lion who visits him each night, until one night he feels sorry for the poor, chilly, smelly lion.

Jarrett, Clare. *Catherine and the Lion.* Carolrhoda Books, 1997. Catherine is comforted by the company of her imaginary lion friend, who goes to school with her and accompanies her in all her at-home activities.

Kleven, Elisa. *The Lion and the Little Red Bird.* Dutton Children's Books, 1992. A little bird discovers why the lion's tail changes color each day.

Lewis, Kim. *Emma's Lamb.* Candlewick Press, 1998. Emma looks after a lost lamb, plays games with him, and helps him find his mother.

Trapani, Iza. *Mary Had a Little Lamb.* Whispering Coyote Press, 1998. This expanded version of the traditional rhyme shows what happens when the lamb decides to go off alone. The last page includes music.

Lion and Lamb Bookmark

Talk about how spring is said to either come in like a lion and go out like a lamb or vice verso before making this bookmark.

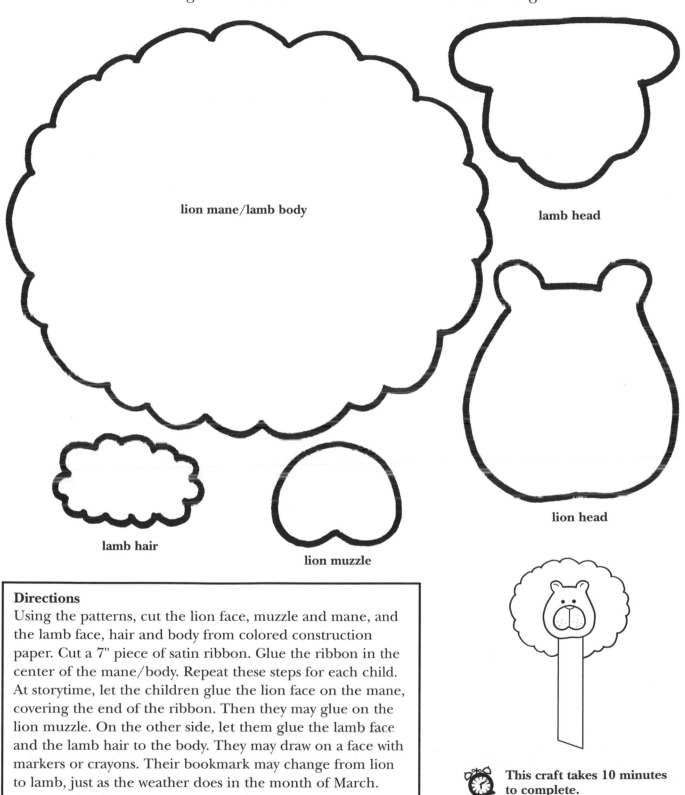

lion mane/lamb body

lamb head

lamb hair

lion muzzle

lion head

Directions
Using the patterns, cut the lion face, muzzle and mane, and the lamb face, hair and body from colored construction paper. Cut a 7" piece of satin ribbon. Glue the ribbon in the center of the mane/body. Repeat these steps for each child. At storytime, let the children glue the lion face on the mane, covering the end of the ribbon. Then they may glue on the lion muzzle. On the other side, let them glue the lamb face and the lamb hair to the body. They may draw on a face with markers or crayons. Their bookmark may change from lion to lamb, just as the weather does in the month of March.

This craft takes 10 minutes to complete.

April Showers

Before Sharing Books

Display a few colorful umbrellas and wear your raincoat and boots. Lead the children in this pantomime. Ask the children to reach into their pocket and take out their invisible raincoat. After everyone puts on their raincoats, have them open up their invisible umbrellas. Now walk in place, looking for a big puddle. Splash in a few little puddles first, and then make a big splash in the big rain puddle. Now lead everyone back indoors. Shake off your umbrellas and fold them up. Shake off your raincoats and hang them up. Sit down for stories.

Rest Activities

Song

Drizzle Song
(*Sung to the tune: "Are You Sleeping"*)
Drip and drizzle,
Drip and drizzle,
April rain,
April rain.
Brr it makes me shiver,
Shudder and quiver.
April rain,
April rain.

Action Rhyme

Rain Walk
A little boy went walking,
(*Walk in place.*)
On a lovely springtime day.
He saw a robin catch a worm,
(*Make a bill with hand.*)
And then it flew away.
(*Hook thumbs together, make hands flutter like wings.*)

He watched a caterpillar crawl,
(*Wiggle finger like a caterpillar.*)
Up the stem of a flower.
Then he splashed all the way home,
(*Stomp feet.*)
In the April rain shower.
(*Fingers wiggle in downward motion like rain.*)

Fingerplay

Raindrops (*Traditional*)

Rain on the housetops,
(*Make a pointed roof with hands.*)
Rain on the trees.
(*Raise arms like tree branches.*)
Rain on the green grass,
(*Point fingers on both hands up.*)
But not on me.
(*Point to self.*)

Books to Share

DeRubertis, Barbara. ***Lucky Duck***. Kane Press, 1997. The other animals try to pull Lucky Duck from a mud puddle he gets stuck in.

Peters, Lisa Westberg. ***Cold Little Duck, Duck, Duck***. Greenwillow Books, 2000. Early one spring a little duck arrives at her pond and finds it still frozen, but not for long.

Serfozo, Mary. ***Rain Talk***. Maxwell Macmillan International, 1993. A child enjoys a glorious day in the rain, listening to the varied sounds it makes as it comes down.

Shannon, George. ***April Showers***. Greenwillow Books, 1995. A group of frogs enjoys dancing in the rain so much that they seem not to notice a snake sneaking up on them.

Stand-up Duck with Umbrella

End your April showers day by helping children make this take-home duck.

Tape or glue here.

Directions

Copy pattern for each child and cut out. Let the children color the picture. Tape the tabs together to make a small circle base so the duck can stand up.

 This craft takes 5 minutes to complete.

Bunnies

Before Sharing Books

Invite a pet store owner to show a baby bunny to the children and talk about how to care for and hold a bunny. Or, display a number of toy bunnies. Use a bunny puppet to show the proper way to hold and care for a bunny.

Rest Activities

Song

In a Cabin in the Woods (*Traditional*)

In a cabin in the woods,
(*Draw a house with fingers.*)
Little man by the window stood.
(*Pretend to look out window.*)
Saw a rabbit running by,
(*Hold up two fingers.*)
Knocking at the door.
(*Pretend to knock.*)
"Help me, help me, help me," he cried.
(*Hands up three times.*)
"Or the hunter will shoot me dead."
(*Pretend to hold a rifle.*)
"Come, little rabbit, come with me.
(*Motion toward yourself.*)
Happy we will be."
(*Hug self.*)

Fingerplays

Funny Little Rabbit (*Traditional*)

Funny little rabbit, (*Hold up two fingers.*)
His tail is soft and white,
Hop, hop, hop goes rabbit, (*Hand hops.*)
All the day and night.

This Little Bunny (*Traditional*)

This little bunny has two pink cycs.
(*Lift one finger for each line.*)
This little bunny is very wise.
This little bunny is soft as silk.
This little bunny is white as milk.
This little bunny nibbles away,
At cabbages and carrots the livelong day.
Polar bears eat 'most anything!
(*Place hands by mouth and pretend to eat.*)

Books to Share

Brown, Margaret Wise. ***Bunn"s Noisy Book.*** Hyperion Books, 2000. A little bunny listens to noises all around him and then makes some of his own.

Jeram, Anita. ***All Together Now.*** Candlewick Press, 1999. Little Duckling and Miss Mouse come to live with Mommy Rabbit and her bunny and enjoy playing all sorts of games with them.

Modesitt, Jeanne. ***Mama, If You Had a Wish.*** Green Tiger Press, 1993. If Little Bunny's mother could have one wish about her child, it would be to keep Little Bunny unchanged and loved by her.

Wells, Rosemary. ***Bunny Cakes.*** Puffin Books, 2000. Max and Ruby spend so much on emergencies while shopping for Grandma's birthday presents, that they just barely have enough money left for gifts.

Bunny Maze

Will the butterfly chase the bunny, or will the bunny hop up to the butterfly?

<hr>

Directions

Enlarge the pattern and make a copy for each child. Have the children trace the paths with their finger first, and then with a crayon. Let the children color the pictures.

 This craft takes 5 minutes to complete.

Springtime

Before Sharing Books

Bring a cutting of spring blossoms from a crab apple tree or other flowering shrub. Ask the children if they have seen flowers growing near their homes. Talk about grass turning green and plants growing. Ask the children to stand up, and comment that they look taller. They must be growing, too!

Rest Activities

Song

Warm Days

(Sung to the tune: "My Bonnie Lies Over the Ocean")

The birds are all making their nests.
The crab apple trees are in bloom.
I unzip my coat when I'm playing.
Warm days are coming soon!
Warm days, warm days,
Warm days are coming soon, real soon.
Warm days, warm days,
Warm days are coming soon.

Action Rhyme

Dandelion Seeds

Dandelions pop up all over the lawn, *(Hop.)*
Showing their sunny faces. *(Hands by face.)*
Then they turn white, and the seeds take flight,
(Spin around.)
Blowing to faraway places. *(Sit down.)*

Fingerplay

Chicks

One, two, three, four, five baby chicks,
(Count fingers.)
Went out on a sunny day.
Four of them scratched in the dust for food,
(Two fingers scratch on palm of other hand.)
And one just wanted to play.
(Fingers run up the arm.)

Books to Share

Fleming, Denise. *In the Tall, Tall Grass.* Henry Holt, 1991. Rhymed text presents a toddler's view of creatures found in the grass from lunchtime till nightfall, such as bees, ants, and moles.

Halls, Kelly Milner. *I Bought a Baby Chicken.* Boyds Mills Press, 2000. When a girl buys a baby chicken, her family buys lots of chicks, too, in this rhyming picture book.

Hunter, Anne. *Possum and the Peeper.* Houghton Mifflin, 1998. When Possum is awakened on the first day of spring by a loud noise that won't stop, he and all the other animals, who have also had their winters' sleep disturbed, set out to discover who is making all the racket.

Kimmel, Eric A. *The Birds' Gift: A Ukrainian Easter Story.* Holiday House, 1999. Villagers take in a flock of golden birds nearly frozen by an early snow and are rewarded with beautifully decorated eggs the next spring.

McBratney, Sam. *The Caterpillow Fight.* Candlewick Press, 1996. A rowdy pillow fight among young caterpillars causes the Big Caterpillar to step in and take action.

Ray, Mary Lyn. *Mud.* Harcourt Brace, 1996. As winter melts into spring, the frozen earth turns into magnificent mud.

Birdhouse

Birds returning to their nesting grounds are a sure sign of spring! Help children make this bird house craft.

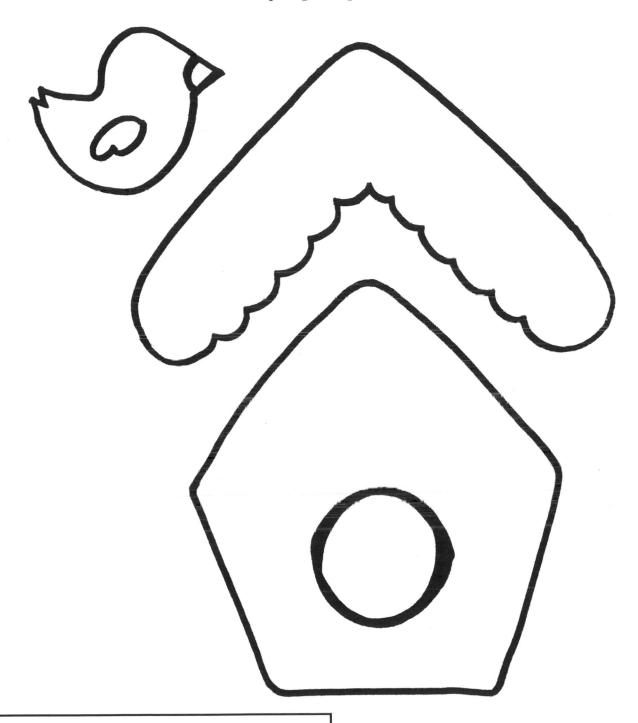

Directions
Copy the pattern pieces on colored paper and cut out for each child. Using a glue stick, let the children place the roof on the birdhouse and the bird by the door.

 This craft takes 5 minutes to complete.

Flowers and Trees

Before Sharing Books

Purchase a marigold or petunia plant. Bring in a branch or piece of bark from a tree. Discuss with the children their favorite colors of flowers, and their favorite activities that involve trees, such as swinging, hide and seek, climbing and having picnics in the shade.

Rest Activities

Action Story

Johnny Climbed a Tree

Johnny climbed a tree in the park one day.
Slowly, slowly, higher and higher.
(*Hand over hand, slowly.*)
He looked around, and what did he see?
(*Place one hand at eyebrows, look left and right.*)
The Ice Cream Truck was coming.
(*Big smile.*)
Quick as a squirrel,
He climbed down, down, down.
(*Hand under hand, quickly.*)
He bought a treat and licked it.
(*Pretend to eat ice cream.*)
Slowly, slowly, because it tasted so good.
It started to drip down his hand,
(*Look at hand.*)
Quick as he could,
He ate it up!
(*Pretend to eat ice cream quickly.*)
Then Johnny looked around,
For another tree to climb.
(*Look left and right.*)

Fingerplay

Five Little Flowers

Five potted flowers in the corner store.
(*Hold up five fingers.*)
A lady came and bought one and then there were four.
Four potted flowers pretty as can be.
(*Hold up four fingers.*)
A lady came and bought one and then there were three.
Three potted flowers, yellow, white, and blue.
(*Hold up three fingers.*)
A lady came and bought one and then there were two.
Two potted flowers became best friends.
(*Hold up two fingers.*)
A lady came and bought them both, and so the story ends.
(*Hold up closed fist.*)
(*Note: You may want to create a visual aid for this action rhyme. Use silk flowers in small pots, or make flannel flowers and use them with a flannel board. Take away one at a time while the rhyme is said.*)

Books to Share

Bunting, Eve. *Flower Garden.* Harcourt Brace Jovanovich, 1994. Helped by her father, a young girl prepares a flower garden as a birthday surprise for her mother.

Goldstone, Bruce. *The Beastly Feast.* Henry Holt, 1998. All sorts of animals bring a variety of foods to share at a picnic: bears bring pears, parrots bring carrots, mosquitoes bring burritos, mice bring rice and so on.

Hall, Zoe. *The Apple Pie Tree.* Scholastic, 1996. Describes an apple tree as it grows leaves and flowers and then produces its fruit, while in its branches robins make a nest, lay eggs and raise a family. Includes a recipe for apple pie.

Hughes, Shirley. *Hiding.* Candlewick Press, 1994. A young girl describes many examples of hiding: children at play, parents reading, the moon behind clouds, flowers underground in winter and the dog at bath time.

Pomeroy, Diana. *Wildflower ABC: An Alphabet of Potato Prints.* Harcourt Brace, 1997. Presents potato-print illustrations for wildflowers for every letter of the alphabet, with all sorts of information about each flower.

Picket Fence Card

Ask children what grows along the fences in their neighborhood. Then, have them make this craft.

Directions
Copy the patterns for the tree trunk, treetop, fence and flowers on colored paper and cut out. Cut blue construction paper or poster board 6" x 9" for each child. Using a glue stick, the children can glue on the pieces to make a card for a gift or for display in their homes.

 This craft takes 10 minutes to complete.

Bees

Before Sharing Books

Using the bee finger puppet, welcome the children to storytime. Let the bee puppet tell the children about his day. For example, he wakes up early, has honey for breakfast, does his chores by gathering pollen from flowers, then for fun he plays tag with the butterflies.

Rest Activities

Song

I Like Honey

(Sung to the tune: "Twinkle, Twinkle Little Star")

I like honey. It's so sweet.
Sticky, yummy, tasty treat.
Spread it on my bread for lunch.
Dip my pretzels. Munch, munch, munch.
I like honey, and I sing,
I like it on everything.

Fingerplay

Here Is the Beehive *(Traditional)*

Here is the beehive, *(Make a fist.)*
Where are the bees?
Hidden away where nobody sees. *(Point to fist.)*
Soon you will see them,
Come out of the hive.
One, two, three, four, five. *(Lift one finger at a time.)*
BZZZZZZ! *(Fingers fly around like bees.)*

Poem

What Do You Do, Bee?

In the morning when the sky is pink,
And the grass is moist with dew,
Do you sleep in awhile, doze and think?
Bee, what do you do?

I get up early, eager to buzz,
And visit colorful flowers.
The dandelions tickle me with their fuzz.
And I laugh, it seems, for hours.

In the heat of the day when the sun is high,
And shade is hard to find.
What do you do, bee? Where do you fly?
Please tell me. Do you mind?

When the sun is hot, I'm at my best.
I work my hardest then.
I fly to the north, and east and west,
To bring the pollen in.

In the evening, when the cricket's hum,
Rustles the leaves on the trees.
What about then? Do you swarm?
Tell me, what is fun for bees?

In the evening, my friends and I,
Dance to the cricket's tune.
We swarm around our cozy hive,
And buzz good night to the moon.

Books to Share

Lewison, Wendy Cheyette. **The Rooster Who Lost his Crow.** Dial Books for Young Readers, 1995. After a bee scares the cock-a-doodle-do out of him, Rooster anxiously searches the entire barnyard for it.

Polacco, Patricia. **In Enzo's Splendid Gardens.** Philomel Books, 1997. A cumulative rhyme describes the uproarious chain of events that ensue when a waiter trips over a book dropped by a boy watching a bee.

Ryder, Joanne. **A Fawn in the Grass.** Henry Holt, 2001. Rhyming text lists a series of animals in their natural habitats, from a fawn in the grass and a snail underneath a leaf to a buzzing bee and two racing hummingbirds.

West, Colin. **"Buzz, Buzz, Buzz," Went Bumblebee.** Candlewick Press, 1996. Bumblebee buzzes around bothering everyone until he comes to a gentle butterfly whom understands that the busy bee is looking for someone to be his friend.

Bee Magnet & Finger Puppet

Talk about the different parts of a bee as you help children make this magnet or finger puppet.

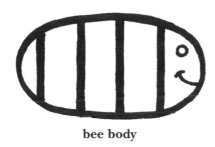

bee body

bee wings

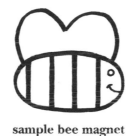

sample bee magnet

finger puppet pattern

Directions

For the bee magnet: Copy the bee body on yellow paper and the heart-shaped bee wings on white paper for each child. Let the children color stripes on the bee body, then glue the wings on the back of the bee body as shown in the illustration. Attach a 1" piece of magnet tape to the back of the bee body.

For the bee finger puppet: Copy the pattern and have the children color the bee. Then tape the tabs to fit each child's finger.

 This craft takes 5 minutes to complete.

Mommy and Me

Before Sharing Books

Bring a picture of yourself as a child and a picture of your mother. Tell about some of the things you liked to do with your mother when you were a child. Display mother and baby puppets or dolls by your books. Ask the children if they like to sing, roller skate, go to the park, etc., with their mother. Ask what else they enjoy doing with and for her.

Rest Activities

Song

Three Little Fishies *(Traditional)*

Down in the meadow in an itty, bitty pool,
Swam three little fishies and a mama fishy, too.
"Swim," said the mama fishy. "Swim if you can."
So they swam and they swam right over the dam.

Clapping Rhymes

My Mommy

My mommy hugs me *(Clap.)* in the morning.
My mommy hugs me *(Clap.)* in the evening.
My mommy hugs me *(Clap.)* in the morning.
That's how I know she loves me.

(Substitute the following words for "hugs": kisses, smiles at, sings to, tickles...)

Mom and Me

While saying this rhyme, do one of the following clap patterns:

Easy way: *Clap hands once, then pat thighs three times. (Repeat.)*

Challenging way: *Face your partner. Clap hands once, cross and clap left hands together. Clap hands once, cross and clap right hands together. (Repeat.)*

Every day, day, day,
I like to play, play, play,
In the sun, sun, sun.
Lots of fun, fun, fun,
Mom and me, me, me,
Happily, lee, lee.
We're together, 'gether, 'gether,
Nothing better, better, better.

Books to Share

London, Jonathan. ***Snuggle Wuggle.*** Silver Whistle, 2000. Text and illustrations describe how various animal mothers cuddle their babies.

McBratney, Sam. ***I'll Always Be Your Friend.*** HarperCollins, 2001. A little fox gets angry and tells his mother, "I'm not your friend anymore," when she tells him it's time to stop playing.

Preller, James. ***Cardinal and Sunflower.*** HarperCollins Publishers, 1998. The seeds scattered by a mother and her child as they walk through the park on a cold winter day feed a pair of cardinals and grow into a plant that feeds their babies the next summer.

Stimson, Joan. ***Big Panda, Little Panda.*** Barron's, 1994. After the arrival of his baby sister, Little Panda's mother begins to call him Big Panda, but it takes him a while to adjust to his new role.

Yolen, Jane. ***How Do Dinosaurs Say Good night?*** Blue Sky Press, 2000. Mother and child ponder the different ways a dinosaur can say good night, from slamming his tail and pouting to giving a big hug and kiss.

Rosebud

After talking about moms, help children make this rose picture for their mom or grandma.

Directions
Copy rosebud on red paper, leaves on green paper and card on white paper for each child, and cut out. Let the children glue the rosebud and leaves on the rose stem.

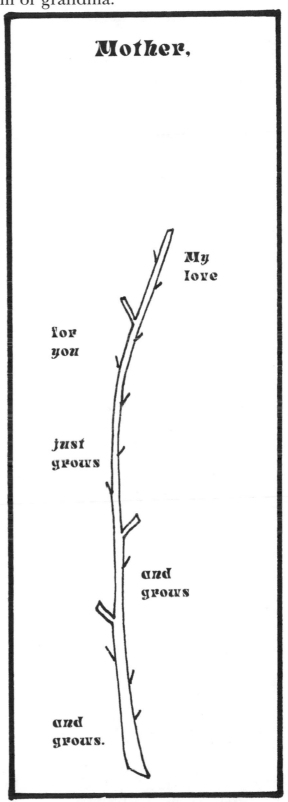

Mother,

My love

for you

just grows

and grows

and grows.

 This craft takes 10 minutes to complete.

Gardens

Before Sharing Books

Show garden gloves, trowel, small rake, pots, seeds and seedlings. Put on the gloves and show how the tools are used. Discuss with the children the kinds of vegetables they like, and what vegetables they may have experienced growing in a garden.

Rest Activities

Song

What Will You Pick Today?

(Sung to the tune: "Row, Row, Row Your Boat")

What will you pick today,
In your garden green?
I will pick a radish today.
The best I've ever seen.

(Substitute the following words for "radish": carrot, pepper, squash, bean…)

Action Rhyme

My Vegetable Garden

In the spring I dig the soil,
(Pretend to dig with a shovel.)
And rake it very fine. *(Pretend to rake the soil.)*
I plant the seeds, one by one.
(Push index finger into opposite hand.)
And hope the sun will shine. *(Arms overhead.)*
I water them, *(Pretend to pour water.)*
I pull the weeds, *(Pretend to pull.)*
And soon the plants come up.
(Push hand up through fist.)
And when the vegetables grow,
I EAT THEM UP! *(Rub tummy.)*

Rhyme

Peas Porridge Hot *(Traditional)*

Peas porridge hot. Peas porridge cold.
Peas porridge in the pot, nine days old.
Some like it hot. Some like it cold.
Some like it in the pot, nine days old.

Books to Share

Hall, Zoe. ***The Surprise Garden.*** Blue Sky Press, 1998. After sowing unmarked seeds, three youngsters wait expectantly for their garden to grow.

King, Christopher. ***The Vegetables Go to Bed.*** Crown, 1994. The tomatoes, carrots, spinach plants and other vegetables in the garden prepare to go to bed, each in its own fashion.

Lobel, Anita. ***Pierrot's ABC Garden.*** Golden Book, 1992. Pierrot brings his friend Pierrette vegetables and other alphabetical gifts, from asparagus to a zebra.

Stevens, Janet. ***Tops and Bottoms.*** Harcourt Brace, 1995. Hare turns his bad luck around by striking a clever deal with the rich and lazy bear down the road.

Vegetable Necklace

After storytime, help children make this take-home reminder of the many different kinds of vegetables.

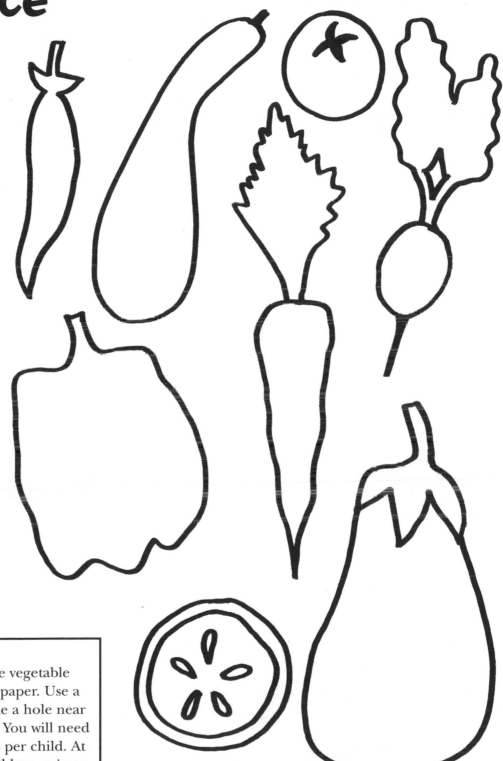

Directions
Copy and cut out the vegetable patterns on colored paper. Use a paper punch to make a hole near the top of each one. You will need five or six vegetables per child. At storytime, let the children string a few vegetables on a 30" piece of yarn. Tie the ends together.

 This craft takes 5 minutes to complete.

Birds

Before Sharing Books

Display a collection of ceramic birds, borrowed from staff, patrons or a local curio shop, or use the bird illustrations in a field guide. Show the birds and tell the children the name of each. Ask them to tell you the colors of each bird.

Rest Activities

Song

The Bird Flew Over the Meadow

(Sung to the tune: "The Bear Went Over the Mountain")

The bird flew over the meadow,
The bird flew over the meadow,
The bird flew over the meadow,
To see what she could see.
And all that she could see,
And all that she could see,
Was the other side of the meadow.
The other side of the meadow,
The other side of the meadow,
Was all that she could see.

Rhyme

Bird Songs

Humming birds hum. Larks trill.
Sparrows cheep on my window sill.
Crows caw, doves coo.
All birds can sing, as children do.

Action Rhyme

Build a Nest

Pick up a twig,
(Bend down to pick up a twig.)
And a piece of string.
(Bend down again.)
Twist them all together,
(Pretend to twist with hands.)
Build a nest that will be warm,
(Circle arms around body.)
In any kind of weather.

Books to Share

Avi. ***The Bird, the Frog, and the Light: A Fable.*** Orchard Books, 1994. A frog learns the truth about his self-importance when he meets a bird whose simple song brings the sun's light to the world.

Berkowitz, Linda. ***Alfonse, Where are You?*** Crown Publishers, 1996. Alfonse the goose can't find Little Bird when they play hide-and-seek, but if he were quiet, he might be able to hear her.

Dunbar, Joyce. ***Baby Bird.*** Candlewick Press, 1998. A bird falls out of his nest while trying to fly and encounters several animals before he finds success.

Massie, Diane Redfield. ***The Baby Beebee Bird.*** HarperCollins Publishers, 2000. The zoo animals find a way to keep the baby beebee bird awake during the day so that they can get some sleep at night.

Winter, Rick. ***Dirty Birdy Feet.*** Rising Moon, 2000. A family's dinnertime is disrupted when a bird flies down the chimney, starting a wild chase across the newly cleaned carpet.

Bird in a Nest

Explain how birds build their nests and lay eggs in them. Then, help the children make this bird/nest craft.

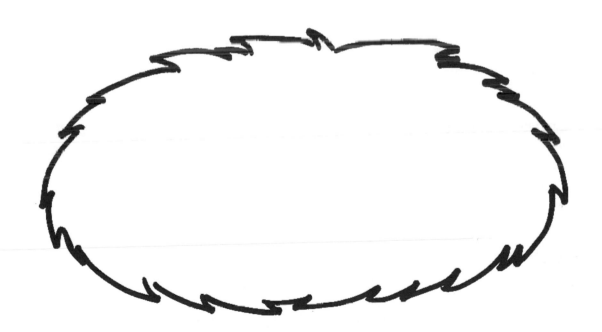

Directions
Copy bird, wing and nest patterns on colored paper and cut out. At storytime, the children can use glue sticks to glue the bird on the nest and the wing on the bird.

 This craft takes 5 minutes to complete.

Bugs and Insects

Before Sharing Books

Purchase ladybugs or praying mantis bugs from a garden supply store, or catch beetles and show them to the children. Ask them to name as many bugs and insects as they can. Discuss with the children whether they think they are beautiful or ugly, useful or harmful, cute or scary.

Rest Activities

Song

Song: I'm a Little Spider

(Sung to the tune: "I'm a Little Teapot")

I'm a little spider. See me crawl.
I can walk right up a wall.
If I climb too high, I just might fall.
But it won't hurt me. Not at all.

Action Rhyme

The Insects and I

I can hop, hop, hop like the grasshoppers do.
(Hop.)
I can wiggle like a caterpillar, can you?
(Wiggle.)
When I stretch out my arms like dragonfly wings,
(Hold out arms.)
I pretend to fly above everything.
Like a roly-poly, I can curl up tight.
(Squat and fold arms over body.)
I can climb on a spider web just right.
(Pretend to climb.)

After pretending to be tiny and wild,
I'm happy to behave like a good little child.
(Sit down.)

Fingerplay

Worm In an Apple

In an apple, in a tree,
(Hands form a ball.)
A tiny worm lived happily.
(Wiggle finger.)
One day he was crawling on a limb,
(Finger wiggles up arm.)
And a bird came along and swallowed him!
(Hand behind back.)

Books to Share

Baranski, Joan Sullivan. *Round Is a Pancake.* Dutton Children's Books, 2001. All around are round things such as a doughnut, a button, a coin, cookies and the spots on a wee ladybug as the townspeople prepare a feast for their king.

Carle, Eric. *The Grouchy Ladybug.* HarperCollins, 1977. A grouchy ladybug who is looking for a fight challenges everyone she meets regardless of their size or strength.

Kirk, David. *Miss Spider's Tea Party.* Callaway Editions: Scholastic, 1994. When lonely Miss Spider tries to

host a tea party, the other bugs refuse to come for fear of being eaten!

Pinczes, Elinor J. *Inchworm and a Half.* Houghton Mifflin, 2001. Several small worms use their varying lengths to measure the vegetables in a garden.

Van Laan, Nancy. *The Big Fat Worm.* Knopf, 1995. A rhythmic read-aloud tale describing a chain of events set in motion when a big fat bird tries to eat a big fat worm.

Clothespin Dragonfly

Explain that some creepy-crawlies are bugs and some are insects. Then, make this dragonfly.

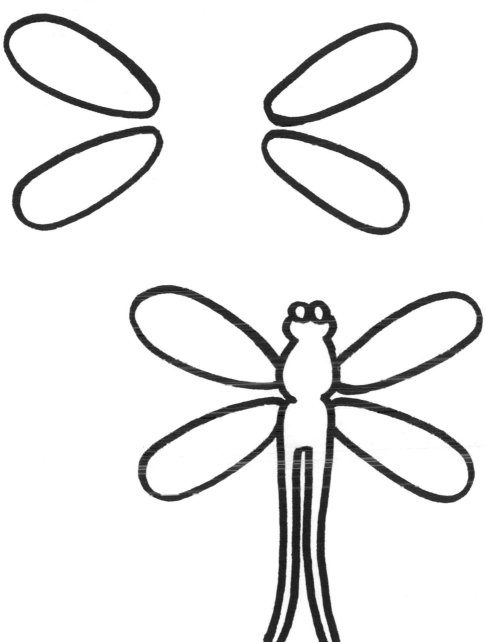

Directions

Copy wing pattern on colored paper and cut out. You will need four per child. Use a paper punch to make small circles for eyes. At storytime, the children may glue the wings and eyes on a clothespin, as shown in the illustration.

 This craft takes 5 minutes to complete.

Daddy and Me

Before Sharing Books

Bring a baseball and glove, a fishing pole, some tools, car washing sponge and other similar items for display. Talk with the children about using these things with Dad. Ask them about chores they help their fathers do at home, and what they like to do with their fathers for fun.

Rest Activities

Song

Daddy's Shoes

(Sung to the tune: "Mary Had a Little Lamb")
Daddy's shoes are very big, very big, very big.
Daddy's shoes are very big and very heavy, too.
(Hold out hands to indicate large size.)
This is how I walk in them, walk in them, walk in them.
This is how I walk in them. I shuffle as I go.
(Take large, slow steps in place.)

Action Rhymes

Playing Catch with Dad

Throw it high,
(Pretend to throw ball overhand.)
Throw it low.
(Pretend to throw ball underhand.)
Throw it fast,
(Pretend to throw a fast pitch.)
Throw it slow.
(Exaggerate a slow-motion pitch.)
I can catch it.
(Slap fist into open hand, as if catching a ball.)

I'm not too bad,
(Point to self.)
When I play catch,
With my dad.
(Smile and look proud.)

Action Story

Piggyback Ride

Up, up, up on Daddy's shoulders.
(Raise hands high overhead.)
I'm going for a ride.
Run fast, run fast.
(Run fast in place.)
Whoa! Slow down.
(Take slow steps in place.)
Duck under the door.
(Squat down.)
Twirl around!
(Turn in a circle.)
Now I'm dizzy.
(Stagger.)
Time to get down.
(Touch the floor.)

Books to Share

Daddy Poems. Selected by John Micklos. Boyds Mills Press, 2000.

Morris, Ann. *The Daddy Book.* Silver Press, 1996. A loving, positive look at fathers around the world and how they relate to their children.

Walters, Virginia. *Are We There Yet, Daddy?* Viking, 1999. A young boy describes the trip he and his father make to Grandma's house, measuring how many miles are left at various points on the trip.

Welch, Willy. *Dancing with Daddy.* Whispering Coyote Press, 1999. Engaged in a joyous dance, a girl and her father leave the house and cause animals and trees to join them in a celebration of life.

Wolf, Jake. *Daddy, Could I Have an Elephant?* Greenwillow Books, 1996. Despite his father's objections, Tony insists on wanting such impractical pets as an elephant, a python, or a flamingo.

Baseball Photo Frame

After storytime, help children create these photo frames to give to Dad or Grandpa.

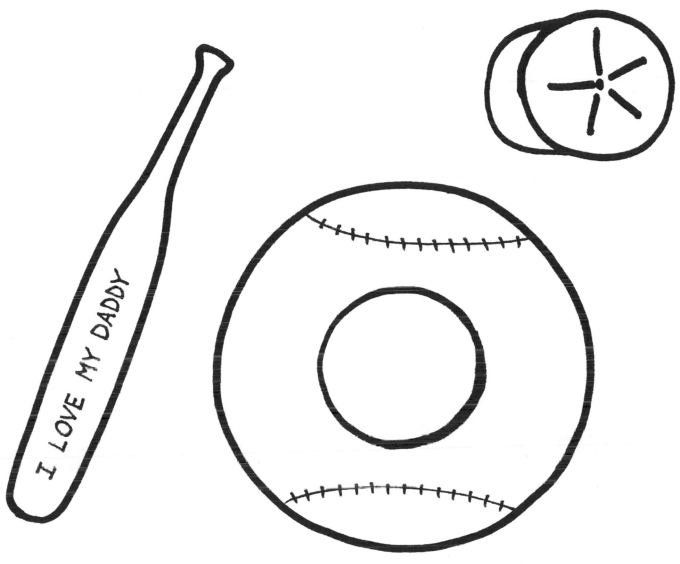

Directions

Copy the baseball on white paper and cut out. Cut out a circle the same size from tagboard. Glue along the lower edge halfway, leaving the top open for sliding in a photo. Copy the baseball bat and cap on colored paper and cut out. The children can glue the bat and cap on the edge of the baseball as shown in the illustration. They may also autograph the baseball. If the children have brought photos with them, they may slide them in.

 This craft takes 10 minutes to complete.

Sunny Days

Before Sharing Books

Come to storytime wearing sunglasses and a brightly colored sun dress or other summer wear. You may wish to decorate the room with lawn furniture. Discuss with the children some of their favorite activities on sunny days, such as visiting the zoo, swimming pool or park.

Rest Activities

Song

Sunny Day Fun

(Sung to the tune: "Mary Had a Little Lamb")

I am going to the zoo, to the zoo, to the zoo.
I am going to the zoo on this sunny day.

(Substitute other places: the pool, the park, for a walk…)

Action Story

Playing In the Sunshine

The sun comes up. *(Arms overhead in a circle.)*
It shines on me. *(Hands come toward face.)*
I put on my hat. *(Hands on head.)*
I put on my sunglasses. *(Fingers circle eyes.)*
I rub on my sunscreen. *(Rub arms.)*
I run through the grass. *(Run in place.)*
I climb a tree. *(Pretend to climb.)*
I run through the sprinkler. *(Run in place.)*
I dry myself off. *(Rub arms.)*
Then I sit down. *(Sit.)*
To have a cool drink. *(Pretend to sip a drink.)*

Poem

My Friend Sunny

Sunny, do you know,
That you make the flowers grow?
That you warm a chilly morning?
That you start the birds singing?
Sunny, come and play.
We'll have lots of fun today.
Chase my shadow, warm a stone,
Melt my ice cream cone.
Sunny, in the night,
Do you feel alone and frightened?
Just think of me if you do.
I'm here, waiting for you.

Books to Share

Blackstone, Stella. *Bear in Sunshine.* Barefoot Books, 2001. Bear likes to play in all kinds of weather.

Bunting, Eve. *Butterfly House.* Scholastic, 1999. With the help of her grandfather, a little girl makes a house for a larva and watches it develop before setting it free, and every summer after that butterflies come to visit her.

Denim, Sue. *The Dumb Bunnies Go to the Zoo.* Blue Sky Press, 1997. When the Dumb Bunnies visit the zoo they let all the animals out of their cages because they mistake a butterfly for an escaped lion.

Lewis, Kim. *One Summer Day.* Candlewick Press, 1996. Little Max wants a closer look at the huge red tractor which passes by his house, so when his friend takes him for a walk to watch it at work, he is delighted.

Rice, Eve. *Swim!* Greenwillow Books, 1996. A young girl describes all the things that she and her father do when they go to the swimming pool each Saturday morning.

Weston, Martha. *Tuck in the Pool.* Clarion Books, 1995. Tuck, a little pig taking swimming lessons, overcomes his fear of the water with the help of his lucky rubber spider.

Sunny Stick Puppet

After children make their puppets, read "My Friend Sunny" while they wave their puppets.

Directions
Copy the patterns on colored paper and cut out, yellow for the face piece and orange for the back piece. At storytime, the children can glue the orange piece to the end of a Popsicle stick. Then they can glue on the yellow piece to finish their stick puppet.

 This craft takes 5 minutes to complete.

Going Fishing

Before Sharing Books

Bring a goldfish in a bowl to storytime. Pretend to hold a fishing pole and cast it out, then have the children cast also. Reel in a fish, about as big as your finger. Repeat, reeling in a fish as big as your hand, your foot, your arm, and as big as you! Now have the children sit down under a shady tree, and get ready for stories.

Rest Activities

Song

Catch a Fish

(Sung to the tune: "London Bridge Is Falling Down")

Catch a fish and throw it back,
Throw it back, throw it back.
Catch a fish and throw it back,
It's too small. (Indicate size with fingers.)
Repeat several times, each time the fish is larger, until finally you sing, "It's too big!"

Action Rhymes

The Fishing Bear

A little bear went fishing,
On a river wide and blue.
He caught a shiny, wiggly fish.
(Reach with hand and grab.)
He caught two. *(Grab another.)*
He ate the shiny, wiggly fish, *(Pretend to eat.)*
He ate the other. *(Pretend to eat.)*
Then he went back to the woods, *(Turn around.)*
To eat berries with his brother.
(Pretend to pick berries.)

Five Fishes

Five little fishes swam in a pool.
(Wiggle hand like a fish.)
They splashed in the water because it made them cool.
(Clap on the word splash.)
They splashed and they splashed for the live-long day,
(Clap twice.)
Then one of the fishes swam away.
(Wiggle hand like a fish.)
(Repeat with four, three, two, one.)

Books to Share

Bauer, Marion Dane. ***When I Go Camping with Grandma.*** BridgeWater Books, 1995. A child enjoys a camping trip with Grandma that includes hiking, canoeing, fishing and cooking out.

Carlstrom, Nancy White. ***Wishing at Dawn in Summer.*** Little, Brown, 1993. A brother and sister express different wishes during an early morning fishing trip.

Hest, Amy. ***Rosie's Fishing Trip.*** Candlewick Press, 1994. Grandpa and Rosie spend the morning fishing and Rosie learns that catching a fish is not the most important thing.

Moore, Elaine. ***Deep River.*** Simon & Schuster Books for Young Readers, 1994. On their first fishing trip together, Grandpa and Jess try to catch a whopper.

Door Hanger

Children love putting signs on their bedroom doors. Help them make this doorknob hanger.

Directions
Enlarge pattern to 115%. Copy pattern and cut out. Allow the children to color the fish, then add tiny round stickers for bubbles. They may hang this on their bedroom door.

 This craft takes 5–10 minutes to complete.

Vacation

Before Sharing Books

Hang travel posters on the walls of your story area. Show postcards from various vacation places, and tell the children about your recent vacation or a dream vacation. Now ask the children to imagine that they will all be going on a vacation together as the stories are read.

Rest Activities

Songs

The Wheels On the Bus *(Traditional)*

The wheels on the bus go round and round,
Round and round, round and round.
The wheels on the bus go round and round,
All through the town.

Additional verses:

The wipers on the bus go swish, swish, swish…
The driver on the bus goes move on back…
The children on the bus go up and down…
The money on the bus goes clink, clink, clink…
The doors on the bus go open and shut…

I'm a Little Postcard

(Sung to the tune: "I'm a Little Teapot")

I'm a little postcard in a store.
Spin me around; I'll fall on the floor.
If I put a stamp right on my face,
The mailman will take me to a faraway place.

Action Rhyme

Beach Vacation

I'm going on vacation, *(Point to self.)*
At a beach in the sun. *(Arms overhead in a circle.)*
I'll do a hula dance, *(Wiggle hips.)*
And build sand castles for fun.
(Bend down, form a castle.)
I'll stretch out my beach blanket, *(Arms out wide.)*
By a coconut tree. *(Arms up like tree branches.)*
And spend the whole summer,
In the sun by the sea. *(Make waves with hand.)*

Books to Share

Root, Phyllis. *Rattletrap Car.* Candlewick Press, 2001. Various disasters threaten to stop Poppa and the children from getting to the lake in their rattletrap car, but they manage to come up with an ingenious solution to each problem.

Smith, Maggie. *Counting Our Way to Maine.* Orchard Books, 1995. On a trip to Maine, the family counts from one baby to twenty fireflies.

Tafuri, Nancy. *The Brass Ring.* Greenwillow Books, 1996. Being on vacation is even more fun for one who is bigger and can do more things such as ride a bike, float and swim, and buy a carousel ticket.

Williams, Garth. *Benjamin's Treasure.* HarperCollins Publishers, 2001. A rabbit gets stranded on a deserted island with a trunk full of treasure and must find his way home.

Palm Tree Picture

After reciting the "Beach Vacation" action rhyme, help children make this palm tree take-along.

Directions
Copy the patterns on colored paper and cut out. At storytime let the children make a beach scene by gluing the palm tree and the sun on blue construction paper. They may draw in water and a sea gull with crayons, if desired.

 This craft takes 5–10 minutes to complete.

Independence Day

Before Sharing Books

Display a flag, and tell the children this is the symbol for the country we live in. Count the red stripes, then count the white stripes. Ask the children to name the colors in the flag. Tell the children that our country will have a birthday party on July 4, and we are all invited. Discuss the fun activities that will be happening in your community to celebrate Independence Day.

Rest Activities

Song

Our Country's Colors

(Sung to the tune: "Three Blind Mice")

Red, White, and Blue,
Red, White, and Blue,
We love you.
We love you.
Our colors waving in the air,
Make us feel proud that we live here.
We'll sing and give a hearty cheer for,
Red, White, and Blue.

Action Rhyme

Watching the Fireworks

We walk together to the park,
When the sky is almost dark.
(Walk in place.)
We spread our blankets on the ground,
And listen for the happy sound.
(Hands pretend to smooth out blanket.)
Soon we hear it. Pop! Pop! Pop!
We hope that it will never stop.
(Put hands by ears.)

Look! The colors flashing bright,
Painting pictures in the night.
(Point up.)
We shout OOO! We shout AHH!
The fireworks look like giant stars.
(Open and close hands several times.)
What a special way to say,
Happy Independence Day!

Fingerplay

Hear the Band Play

(Hold up five fingers. Touch one at a time while saying the rhyme.)

One drummer played boom boom boom,
Two trumpets played ta ta ta,
Three flutes played tweedle dee dee,
Four clarinets played waddle dee day,
Five happy children shouted hooray!

Books to Share

Bates, Katharine Lee. *America the Beautiful.* Atheneum, 1993. An illustrated edition of the nineteenth-century poem, later set to music, celebrating the beauty of America.

Beat the Drum Independence Day Has Come: Poems for the Fourth of July. Selected by Lee Bennett Hopkins; illustrations by Tomie de Paola. Wordsong, 1993. An anthology of poems about American independence.

Thomas, Jane Resh. *Celebration!* Hyperion Books for Children, 1997. Grandmother, aunts and uncles, and assorted cousins gather for the annual picnic in Maggie's backyard, complete with good food and family fun.

Ziefert, Harriet. *Hats Off for the Fourth of July!* Viking, 2000. Spectators wait to see what will come next as they watch the town's Fourth of July parade.

U.S.A. Bear

These patriotic bears will be a hit with the children!

Directions
Copy the patterns and cut out. Let the children color the bear, the bow tie, the banner and the stars. They may glue them on the bear using a glue stick. This bear may be hung in a window or on the refrigerator to show patriotism.

 This craft takes 10 minutes to complete.

Trains

Before Sharing Books

Ask someone in your community to set up a model train for storytime. Let the children watch it go around the track for a few minutes. Lead the children in making the sound of a train whistle. Tell them that means the train is coming into the station, so they must get ready for storytime.

Rest Activities

Song

Song: Down by the Station (*Traditional*)

Down by the station, early in the morning,
See the little puff-a-bellies all in a row.
See the stationmaster pull the little handle,
Puff, puff, toot, toot, off we go.

Action Story

Train Ride

I put on my jacket. (*Zip jacket.*)
I put on my shoes. (*Pull on shoes.*)
I pick up my suitcase. (*Hold handle of suitcase.*)
I run to the station. (*Run in place.*)
I listen for the train whistle. (*Hold hand to ear.*)
I look down the track. (*Hold hand above eyes.*)
Oh, boy! The train is coming. (*Jump up excitedly.*)
I get on board. (*Step in place.*)
I sit by the window. (*Pretend to sit.*)
I bounce, clickety clack, as the train speeds away.
(*Bounce.*)

Poem

The Little Train

Toot, toot, toot. Around the track.
The little train goes clickety-clack.
Away it goes, then it comes back.
Clickety-clack, clickety-clack.

Books to Share

Lewis, Kevin. *Chugga-chugga Choo-choo.* Hyperion Books for Children, 1999. A rhyming story about a toy freight train's day, from loading freight in the morning to retiring to the roundhouse after the day's work is done.

Spence, Robert, III. *Clickety Clack.* Viking, 1999. A train gets noisier and more crowded as quacking ducks, dancing acrobats, talking yaks and packs of elephants board.

Sturges, Philemon. *I Love Trains!* HarperCollins Publishers, 2001. A boy expresses his love of trains, describing many kinds of train cars and their special jobs.

Wormell, Christopher. *Puff, Puff, Chugga-chugga.* Margaret K. McElderry Books, 2001. Puff, puff, chugga, chugga here comes the little train, which ends up holding many big passengers.

Train on a Circle Track

Make a choo-choo train at the end of your storytime.

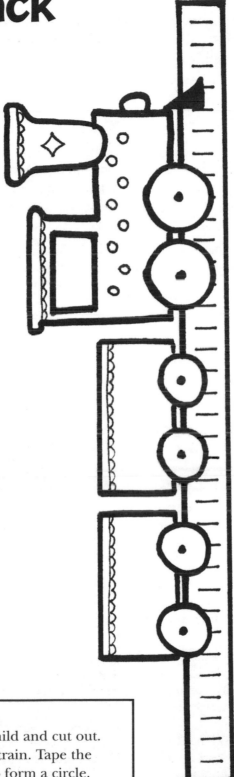

Directions
Copy the pattern for each child and cut out.
Allow the child to color the train. Tape the
ends of the track together to form a circle.
The train will stand up.

 This craft takes 10 minutes to complete.

Picnics

Before Sharing Books

Spread blankets on the floor in your storytime area. Have a picnic basket nearby. You may wish to hand out a paper plate or napkin to each child. Let them imagine their favorite picnic lunch. Is it peanut butter sandwiches? Is it cold chicken? Is it macaroni salad? While they are pretending to eat, begin your stories.

Rest Activities

Song

Yummy Yummy

(Sung to the tune: "London Bridge Is Falling Down")

Yummy, yummy chocolate cake,
Chocolate cake, chocolate cake.
Yummy, yummy chocolate cake,
At the Picnic!
Substitute new foods, such as: hard boiled eggs, ham and cheese, carrot sticks, lemonade…

Action Rhyme

The Squirrel's Picnic

Two little squirrels, high in the tree.
(Raise arms high.)
Are waiting for the picnic at half past three.
(Hands by face like paws.)
The school bell rings. The children come.
(Hold up 10 fingers.)
They give the squirrels peanuts. Yum, yum, yum.
(Rub tummy.)

Poem

Picnic Ants

The picnic ants are hungry.
What do they smell?
Delicious pie, sandwiches,
And sweet pickles as well.
They're marching to your table,
All in a line.
If you feed them several crumbs,
They'll feel just fine.

Books to Share

Alborough, Jez. *It's the Bear!* Candlewick Press, 1994. Eddie and his mom go into the woods for a picnic and meet a very large, very hungry bear.

Inkpen, Mick. *Picnic.* Harcourt, 2001. Kipper and Tiger plan a picnic, which is nearly ruined by a series of disruptions.

Prater, John. *Once Upon a Picnic.* Candlewick Press, 1996. While Mom and Dad do nothing but daydream at the picnic, the young boy keeps very active noticing all kinds of things going on around them.

Woodson, Jacqueline. *We Had a Picnic this Sunday Past.* Hyperion Books for Children, 1997. A young girl describes her various relatives and the foods they bring to the annual family picnic.

Fruit Pie

Ask children what kind of fruit pie is their favorite, then help them make this fruit pie take-along.

Directions

Copy the piecrust pattern on white paper for each child. Copy the peach slices and cherries on colored paper and cut out about 10 for each child. At storytime the children can color the piecrust golden brown, then glue on the fruit to complete their pie.

 This craft takes 10 minutes to complete.

The Beach

Before Sharing Books

Bring an assortment of seashells for display. Ask each child to pack a pretend bag with things they will need at the beach. They may suggest putting in a beach towel, a hat, a radio for listening to music, a pail and shovel for digging in the sand, and sandals for their feet. When everyone is packed, walk in place until you come to a good place on the beach, then sit down for stories.

Rest Activities

Song

Swimming At the Beach
(Sung to the tune: "Baa, Baa Black Sheep")

Grab your towel, grab a ball.
Let's go swimming, one and all.
Count the waves, one by one.
Have a good time in the sun.
Grab your towel, grab a ball.
Let's go swimming, one and all.

Sandy Feet
(Sung to the tune: "Head, Shoulders, Knees and Toes")

Sandy shoulders, sandy knees, sandy feet.
Sandy shoulders, sandy knees, sandy feet.
Brush the sand off. Let's be neat.
Sandy shoulders, sandy knees, sandy feet.

Poem

Sand Castle

I'm going to build a castle,
With towers tall and straight.
I'll dig a moat around it,
With a drawbridge and a gate.
My castle will have windows,
Each with a lovely view.
In the dungeon I will have,
A dragon or two.
I'll host a royal banquet,
Elegant and grand.
I'm going to build a castle.
A castle made of sand.

Books to Share

Hayles, Marsha. *Beach Play.* Henry Holt, 1998. The sunny beach offers many fun and exciting activities for those who spend a day playing on its warm sands and in the water.

Roosa, Karen. *Beach Day.* Clarion Books, 2001. Rhyming text describes a perfect day at the beach, complete with sandy knees, deviled eggs and a castle with a moat.

Ryan, Pam Muñoz. *Hello, Ocean!* Charlesbridge, 2001. Using rhyming text, a child describes the wonder of the ocean experienced through each of her five senses.

Selby, Jennifer. *Beach Bunny.* Harcourt Brace, 1996. Because of careful preparation, Harold the bunny enjoys an active morning at the beach, but the outing is almost ruined when he thinks that he forgot to prepare for lunch.

Seashells on the Beach

Talk about "hearing the ocean" in a seashell, then help children make this scene.

Directions

Purchase a sheet of sandpaper for each child. Copy the seashell patterns and cut out. Let the children color the seashells and glue them on the sandpaper.

 This craft takes 10 minutes to complete.

It's Hot!

Before Sharing Books

Talk to the children about their favorite ways to cool off in hot weather. You may show a small electric fan, a folded paper fan, a squirt bottle, a tall drink, a small wading pool....

Rest Activities

Action Rhyme

It's Too Hot

It's too hot to wear long pants, long pants,
(Bend down and touch feet on the word "long.")
It's too hot today.
(Fan face with hand.)
It's too hot to wear long pants, long pants,
(Bend down and touch feet.)
When I go out to play.
(Point thumb, indicating going out.)
It's just right to wear short pants, short pants,
(Pat thighs on the word "short.")
It's just right today.
(Touch finger to thumb in the OK sign.)
It's just right to wear short pants, short pants,
(Pat thighs.)
When I go out to play.
(Point thumb, indicating going out.)

Clapping Rhyme

It's Going To Be Hot

(On the three repeated words in each line, cross arms and pat shoulders twice, clap twice, pat lap twice.)

It's going to be hot, hot, hot,
Ready or not, not, not.

I'm going to get cool, cool, cool,
Down at the pool, pool, pool.
It feels so nice, nice, nice,
Sucking on ice, ice, ice.
Get a cool drink, drink, drink,
Quick as a wink, wink, wink.

Fingerplay

Two Little Piggies

Two little piggies sat in the sun.
(Hold up two fingers.)
"Hi," said this one.
(Wiggle one finger.)
"Hi," said that one.
(Wiggle other finger.)
"Hot!" said this one.
(Wiggle one finger.)
"Hot!" said that one.
(Wiggle other finger.)
So they ran to the puddle,
(Hands behind back.)
To cool off and have some fun.

Books to Share

Bauer, Marion Dane. ***Bear's Hiccups.*** Holiday House, 1998. On a hot summer day, while Bear and Frog are arguing about who owns the cool, wet pond, Frog disappears and Bear develops a sudden case of hiccups.

Cousins, Lucy. ***Maisy's Pool.*** Candlewick Press, 1999. Maisy the mouse and her animal friends cool off on a hot day in Maisy's wading pool.

Crews, Nina. ***One Hot Summer Day.*** Greenwillow Books, 1995. Relates a child's activities in the heat of a summer day punctuated by a thunderstorm.

Havill, Juanita. ***Treasure Nap.*** Houghton Mifflin, 1992. On an afternoon when it is too hot to sleep, a young girl asks to hear the story about how her great-great-grandmother came to the United States from Mexico, bringing a special treasure.

Soda Straw Pals

Create these fun straw pals, then serve juice in small cups so children can try out their craft.

Directions
Copy the patterns and cut out. Punch holes with a paper punch. Have children pick a pattern and color, then insert a soda straw through the holes.

 This craft takes 5 minutes to complete.

Water Play

Before Sharing Books

Ask the children to name some animals that live near the water. Lead the children in hopping like a frog, splashing like a fish, crawling like a turtle, etc. Ask the children to imagine that the storytime room is a cool pond. Now ask the children to pretend they are going to sit on their own lily pad and listen to stories.

Rest Activities

Song

Splash and Play

(Sung to the tune: "Mary Had a Little Lamb")

Do you like to splash and play,
Splash and play, splash and play.
Do you like to splash and play,
In your swimming pool?

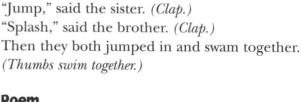

Fingerplay

Two Little Frogs

Two little frogs by a little pond of water.
(Hold up thumbs.)
One was a sister and one was a brother.
(Wiggle one thumb, then the other.)

"Jump," said the sister. *(Clap.)*
"Splash," said the brother. *(Clap.)*
Then they both jumped in and swam together.
(Thumbs swim together.)

Poem

Wiggley, Wrigglcy, Giggley Fish

Down in the deepest part of the pool,
Five little fishes swim in a school.
Four of them swim all in a line,
But one little fish, who was feeling fine,
Swam in a squiggle, swam in a swirl,
Swam in a zigzag, swam in a curl.
He said, "Follow me, if you wish,"
That wiggley, wriggley, giggley fish.
Soon the others were feeling fine,
Much too fine to swim in a line.
They swam in a squiggle, swam in a swirl,
Swam in a zigzag, swam in a curl.
Now the whole school swims splash, splosh, splish,
Wiggley, wriggley, giggley fish.

Books to Share

Berger, Barbara. *A Lot of Otters.* Philomel Books, 1997. As a lot of otters wrestle, roll, and cavort on the water, they make such a commotion of light that Mother Moon finds her lost child.

Ford, Miela. *Bear Play.* Greenwillow Books, 1995. Two polar bears play in the water.

Kelly, Irene. *Ebbie and Flo.* Smith & Kraus, 1997. Flo is a daredevil salmon while her brother Ebbie is a more cautious fish, but during their journey down river to the sea, they come to appreciate the differences in their personalities.

Martin, Bill. *The Happy Hippopotami.* Harcourt Brace Jovanovich, 1991. The happy hippopotami enjoy a merry holiday at the beach, wearing pretty beach pajamas, dancing the maypole or battling with water guns.

Simmons, Jane. *Come Along, Daisy!* Little, Brown, 1997. Daisy the duckling becomes so engrossed in playing with dragonflies and lily pads that she temporarily loses her mother.

Frog On a Lily Pad

After reciting the "Two Little Frogs" fingerplay, help children make this frog take-away.

Directions
Copy the pattern and cut out. Let the children color, then paste the frog on the lily pad with a glue stick.

 This craft takes 10 minutes to complete.

Boats

Before Sharing Books

Bring in a variety of toy boats to show. Talk about what makes the boats move. Some move with sails, and need wind. Some move with a motor, and need fuel. Some move with oars, and need people to row them. Sing "Row, Row, Row Your Boat," and pretend to row. Now have everyone pretend to row the boat to shore, tie it up, and sit quietly for stories.

Rest Activities

Song

Sailing

(Sung to the tune: "Baa, Baa, Black Sheep")

Sailing, sailing on the lake.
Watch that speedboat, watch that wake.
Turn the sail, catch the breeze.
Glide along, sail with ease.
Daylight fading, clouds are thin.
Sailing, sailing back again.

Action Story

A Sea Cruise

(Allow the children to pantomime the actions any way they wish.)

We get on our ship.
Friends call, Bon Voyage.
We wave good-bye.
We feel the ocean mist on our faces.
We watch the ships at port get smaller and smaller.
We see blue water all around us.
We spot some dolphins leaping beside us.
We enjoy going fast!

Time to dress up for dinner.
We order wonderful food.
We watch a musical show.
We go to our cabin.
We get tucked in bed.
We dream about a fun day tomorrow.

Fingerplay

Boat Count

(Start by holding up five fingers. Make the noise of each kind of boat. Take away one finger at a time until you get to one.)

Five motorboats go zoom, zoom, zoom!
Four canoes go slosh, slosh, slosh!
Three sailboats go glide, glide, glide!
Two kayaks go swish, swish, swish!
One toy boat goes putter, putt, putt!

Books to Share

Crews, Donald. *Sail Away.* Greenwillow Books, 1995. A family takes an enjoyable trip in their sailboat and watches the weather change throughout the day.

Jewell, Nancy. *Sailor Song.* Clarion Books, 1999. A mother sings her child a song that describes how a sailor makes his way home from the sea to his family.

Titherington, Jeanne. *Baby's Boat.* Greenwillow Books, 1992. Describes a baby falling asleep as sailing out in a silver moon boat.

Vischer, Phil. *How Many Veggies?* Tommy Nelson, 1997. Bob the tomato is joined by nine other vegetables until his boat becomes so full that it begins to sink.

Waddell, Martin. *Sailor Bear.* Candlewick Press, 1992. Lost and lonely, a little bear embarks on a rather perilous sailing venture, but winds up with his heart's desires realized.

Sailor Hat

After children have made their sailor hats, have them put them on. Then, lead them in singing the "Sailing" song.

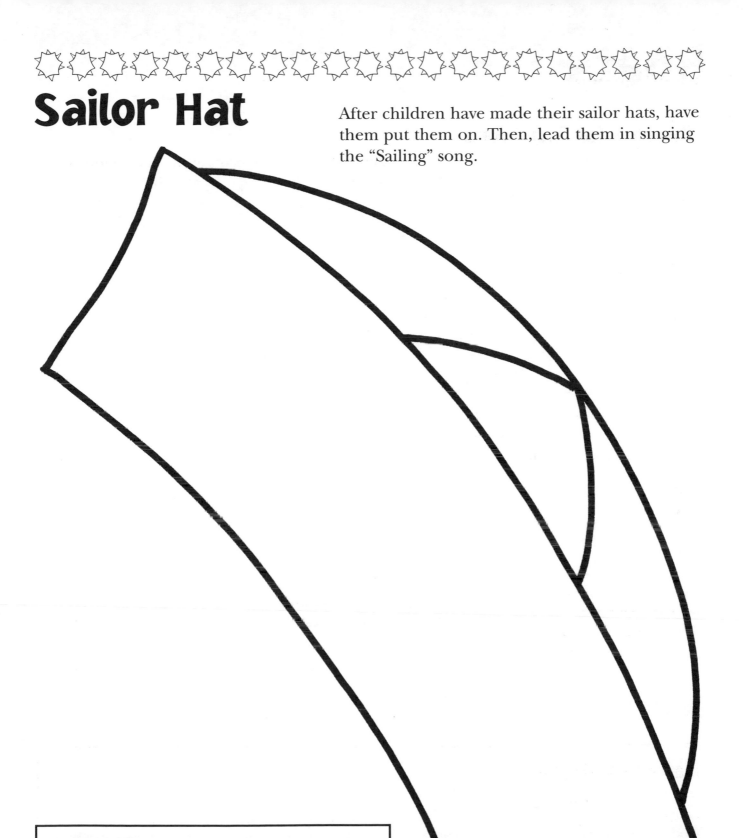

Directions
Copy the pattern on white paper and cut out. Cut a strip of white paper 14" x 1". At storytime, let each child write his/her name on the hat and decorate it with crayons. Tape the paper strip to sides of hat, adjusting to fit each child.

 This craft takes 5 minutes to complete.